Better Than Normal

DR. DALE ARCHER

*HOW WHAT MAKES
YOU DIFFERENT CAN
MAKE YOU EXCEPTIONAL*

Better Than Normal

 CROWN ARCHETYPE • NEW YORK

DISCLAIMER

I have changed the names, as well as certain identifying details, of most of the people whose stories appear in this book, in order to protect their privacy. All of the stories, however, are based on the cases of real patients, people I know, or people whom my research team either interviewed or learned about through reliable secondary sources. Although I have done my best to provide the most thorough and careful discussion of personality traits and conditions, this book should not be considered in any way a substitute for professional medical advice and/or treatment.

Copyright © 2012 by Dale Archer

All rights reserved.

Published in the United States by Crown Archetype, an imprint of the Crown Publishing Group, a division of Random House, Inc., New York.
www.crownpublishing.com

Crown Archetype with colophon is a trademark of Random House, Inc.

Library of Congress Cataloging-in-Publication Data

Archer, Dale.
Better than normal : how what makes you different can make you exceptional /
Dale Archer. — 1st ed.
1. Personality. 2. Personality disorders. 3. Individual differences. I. Title.
BF698.A722 2012
155.2'32—dc23   2011026427

ISBN 978-0-307-88746-7
eISBN 978-0-307-88747-4

Printed in the United States of America

BOOK DESIGN BY ELINA NUDELMAN
JACKET DESIGN BY JEAN TRAINA
JACKET PHOTOGRAPHS: © GETTY IMAGES
AUTHOR PHOTOGRAPH: STEPHANIE JONES

10 9 8 7 6 5 4 3 2

FIRST EDITION

To all of us who are different . . .

CONTENTS

Better Than Normal

INTRODUCTION

"Doctor, am I normal?"

As a psychiatrist, I hear this question over and over again—far more than you might imagine. I hear it from friends, family members, patients, recent acquaintances, and folks I've just met for the first time. In today's world, people wonder whether what they think, feel, and believe—or how they act—is considered "normal."

What do we mean by "normal," and what's so great about normal anyway? We are taught as children that we all have certain talents and abilities that make us special. If being normal means being just like everyone else, where's the fun in that? Shouldn't we prefer to be unique and embrace who and what we are?

When it comes to our mental health, though, we still worry:

If I'm a little impatient and sometimes have a short attention span, does that mean I have attention deficit disorder?

Because I have high self-esteem and like it when others pay attention to me, does that make me a narcissist?

What if I have occasional mood swings? Could I be bipolar?

The answer to these questions, for most people, is no, no, *no!*

Yet there are a handful of personality traits that can be a part of a normal character but that *when present in the extreme* can be abnormal and cause people trouble and even elicit a psychiatric diagnosis. These are the traits that people worry about the most, but they are also the very traits that define who we are. They are the traits that have the potential to make us genuinely special—and even great.

This book is about the eight most common, and most important, of these traits. (It's important to say that most of us have many, even all, of these traits to some degree.) It's about learning to identify which traits are dominant. It's about recognizing how those traits can cause you trouble. And, most important, it's about learning how you can put your dominant traits to work for you.

For example:

Have you found a way to put your adventurous nature to focused and productive use? Or does it propel you dizzily from one activity to the next, never finishing what you start?

Have you been able to make your perfectionism fulfilling and valuable? Or does it more often feel like an obsession that's overwhelming to you and frustrates others?

How about your anxiety? Does it spur you into action or disable you with fear?

Looking closely at your personality profile can be a scary thing. At first, you might not like what you see. It may make you worry about yourself or about others around you—a child, a spouse, a friend, or a colleague. You may compare yourself to the horror stories portrayed in the media of seemingly ordinary people who turn out to be "crazy." You begin to wonder if perhaps you should be evaluated, or go to therapy, or even take medication to help tone down that perfectionism or rein in the adventurousness or replace magical thinking with a more logical approach so you'll be more like everyone else and be normal. Or at least more like what you think the normal person should look like.

I have been considering these questions with my patients for twenty-five years. And I have also asked *myself* these questions, especially at critical turning points in my life and my career. I know that they can be difficult because they usually involve change, which means contemplating a new way of thinking and being. Many times it feels easier to struggle along with "normal" than to take the leap and embrace who we really are.

For me, one of those periods of questioning came in the summer of 2008 in, of all places, Las Vegas. But the story begins in Lake Charles, Louisiana.

In 1987 I had just finished my psychiatry residency. With my wife and two kids, I moved back to Lake Charles, a beautiful little town just west of New Orleans, where I was born. I grew up in Lake Charles, my parents still lived there, and I had decided to establish my psychiatric practice there. I remember the tremendous excitement that came from starting my own clinic. My adventurous nature made me eager to try out fresh ideas and provoke changes in the profession. In short, I felt ready to make a difference and to try to change the world.

I'd only been in town a few weeks when I got a call from Jan Hardy, the anchor of a local TV news program. She explained that she was doing a series on health issues and wanted me to come on her show and talk about—and this is where she caught me by surprise—depression. People didn't talk about depression very much in those days. But Jan sounded smart and nice and knowledgeable on the topic, so I said sure.

A pretty amazing thing happened when Jan and I got on the air together. Not long after she started the interview, Jan revealed that she herself suffered from depression. Not only that, she told the world that she was taking Prozac, one of the early antidepressant medications. (The drug became world famous in 1993, the year that Peter Kramer published his bestselling book *Listening to Prozac.*)

Today, no one thinks much about it if you admit you're on meds for depression. (In fact, in some circles, they may be surprised if you say you're not.) But, in Louisiana, in 1987, it was a huge admission for anyone to make, let alone a TV personality, and on a live show no less. It was a bombshell, really. Depression, in fact any kind of mental illness, carried a real stigma at the time. It was okay to be a little down, sure, but flat-out, can't-function depressed? That was not something most people would admit to.

Jan's revelation sparked an interesting dialogue between us on air. I said that the medical community had learned a lot about depression in the past few years. That we had come to think of it as a medical condition, caused by a chemical imbalance in the brain. And just like any other medical condition—diabetes, heart disease, high blood pressure—depression could be successfully treated with medicines. Prozac, while the best known at the time, was just one of several antidepressants available.

After the show, Jan told me she thought it had gone really well. A few days later, she called me again and said that she had gotten a lot of positive responses from her viewers as well as from the station management. She asked if I'd be interested in doing a regular appearance on her news program. "I've been stigmatized because I have depression," she told me. "I'm sure others have too. I'd love you to talk about how psychiatric problems like these come about as the result of a medical condition."

For the next two years, Jan and I did a five-minute segment every Monday at noon. I'd talk a little bit about the latest findings related to depression, bipolar disorder, OCD, and other mental health conditions and then we'd take comments and questions from viewers. It was new ground for the people of Lake Charles, Louisiana, in the late eighties, and it was considered a big deal.

Not only was that the start of my media career, it gave me a better understanding of my own dominant traits. I saw that the combination of confidence, along with the pleasure I take in helping others on a much larger scale, could bring me fulfillment beyond the clinical practice of psychiatry. I wrote a book, *Chemical Imbalance Depression*. I began to give talks and conduct seminars for various groups and associations, mostly in Louisiana and Texas.

I continued to build my practice. Life was filled and fulfilling. My dominant traits were fully and appropriately engaged.

I was working full time at my clinic, making weekly television appearances, caring for my family, and pursuing a series of hobbies. I loved sailing and bicycling, and I rode a motorcycle. And, although not many of my colleagues know this, I became a world-class poker player.

It turns out that my personality profile is highly suited to playing poker. Or to use more technical language, my dominant personality traits give me the ascendant strengths that make me tough competition at the poker table. I'm just narcissistic enough to be confident in myself when the odds aren't looking good, and to be resilient on the days when luck lets me down. And like many competitive people, I'm a magical thinker. Often thought of as a combination of intuition and faith, magical thinking, along with my years as a psychiatrist, is what enables me to read my opponents like a book. I can instantly get a feel for what cards they're holding and whether they're bluffing.

I became involved in poker for an unusual reason. I have always had an ability to tell when another person is being truthful (classic magical thinking) and decided to try out poker as a test. For several years, I played poker quite seriously. I competed a few times in the World Series of Poker, a six-week serial tournament that culminates in the Main Event, considered the World Championship of Poker. In 2004, I played in the Main Event and placed eleventh in the world.

Then I hit a bumpy patch—in my personal life, in my professional career, and in poker.

I got divorced in 2006. My two great kids were all grown up and away at school. And for reasons that I'll describe in a moment, I seemed to have lost that feeling of fulfillment that I once got from my work at the clinic and my television show.

So not long after the divorce was final, I decided I'd play poker on a professional level, albeit for all the wrong reasons. Why not? I had a good track record, had won tournaments and made some money. I thought that I could answer the question "What does normal mean for me now?" in a new and exciting way.

I stuck it out for two years, but by the time the World Series of Poker Main Event rolled around in May 2008, I was pretty convinced that the poker-playing life was not for me. Still, I decided to give it one last go. I flew to Las Vegas, checked into the hotel, and tried to get myself in a winning frame of mind. Nothing doing. It didn't take long for me to bust out—which meant I was out of chips, out of luck, and out of the tournament for the year.

At the end of the day, I left the casino and made a beeline for Petrossian, the well-known Russian piano bar at the Bellagio Hotel. I grabbed a table and decided to treat myself to a glass of champagne. While I sipped my drink, I listened to the pianist and thought things over.

Okay, I thought, *poker is fun, especially when I win big, but no way can it be my next career. It can be a hobby, sure, but I've had my little experiment and now it's time to get serious. Poker brought out the worst of my best characteristics. So, what do I want to do next with my skills? Where do I want to go? What can I do that is truly meaningful—and that is genuinely me?*

I realized that my disaffection was caused, at least in part, by the changes that had taken place in the field of psychiatry during the previous decade. Throughout the 1990s, as my practice grew and I took on partners and we became more and more widely known and successful, I had continued to speak out about depression. I wanted to help the millions of people like Jan Hardy who had been stigmatized because of their condition. Considering the number of estimated cases of depression across the country, it seemed obvious to me that we had a national crisis on our hands.

Of course, mine was only one of many voices in this conversation. Gradually the word got out and acceptance started to build. So much so that by 2003 or so, my practice—and the practice of psychiatry in general—looked very different than it had in 1987.

How so? Twenty years ago, people went to a psychiatrist only when they were really in trouble. They were severely depressed, manic, or psychotic. They couldn't function. A shrink was the last resort.

But now, many of the patients I was seeing would hardly have qualified as "patients" at all when I started out. This is not to say they weren't dealing with difficult issues, but they often didn't require extensive treatment or medication. I remember one patient who came to see me soon after his mom died. He was feeling sad, down, and depressed. I went through the routine questions.

"Are you sleeping all right?" I asked.

"Yes, I sleep okay."

"How's your energy level?"

"It's good."

"Are you able to work?"

"Sure, I go to work every day. My boss and coworkers are the best."

"Are you eating well?"

"My diet hasn't really changed." He sighed. "I'm just really, really sad."

"Well, it's only been a week since your mom passed away," I said. "It's normal to feel sad, even depressed, after a parent dies. I don't see that you have any clinical problems. You don't seem to have any physical criteria. I don't think there's any need for medication. In fact, my sense is that you're dealing with this amazingly well. Grieving is a natural part of life. When we lose people we love, it's very hard to deal with."

He sighed again. "Yes, it is. I just thought maybe some medicine would help. You know, like an antidepressant?"

So we talked for a while about how to focus on the good times with his mom and ways to celebrate her memory and her life. Then I told him, "Why don't you give it a month and see how things go? If anything gets worse, I'm here. Come back and we'll reevaluate."

He didn't come back. In fact, I bumped into him a few months later and he said, "The best thing you told me was that I didn't need medicine, that what I was going through was normal. I worked through everything and though I still get sad from time to time, I'm in good shape."

By 2008, that kind of visit had become the norm rather than the exception. And in addition to this increase in the number of visits from people who were *not* severely ill, I saw another trend: an increase in the number of people who came to me with prescription drug abuse issues, including Ritalin, Adderall, Xanax, and most notably, narcotic painkillers. The abuse of serious pain medications such as Oxycontin, Lorcet, Lortab, Percocet, and Percodan was seriously on the rise, not just in my neck of the woods, but nationwide. Folks were abusing and becoming addicted to the very same legal prescription drugs that we used to treat psychiatric and medical problems. It was reaching near-epidemic proportions.

Sitting there at the bar in Las Vegas, I articulated more clearly the thoughts that had been gathering for some time.

Not only have we destigmatized the issue of mental health, I realized, but we've gone completely in the other direction. We've actually glamorized it. Today it seems that everybody needs to see a mental health professional. Everyone needs to be evaluated. We all need to be treated for something.

Let me quickly state that I believe it's a positive thing that so many people have become aware of their own mental health, and the issue in general, and are interested in talking about and addressing a wide range of emotional and psychological concerns. On the other hand, however, I realized then that we were clearly going down the wrong path, and a potentially dangerous one, by seeing mental health issues everywhere. Overevaluating. Overdiagnosing. And, most important of all, overmedicating.

And it wasn't only a matter of an overreliance on medication. I saw that traditional therapy, too, was in need of redirection. Don't get me wrong, I'm a big advocate of the talking cure, and always have been. After all, I've spent nearly thirty years helping patients, with a combination of talk and meds. But, increasingly, I saw that therapy was being applied just as meds were—to "fix" what seemed to be abnormal traits. So, if a patient went to a therapist because she thought of herself as shy, the almost automatic response had become, "Let's work together to make you bolder and more assertive and outgoing!" A better way would be to start by considering the patient's strengths. Maybe they could be better understood and accentuated? Maybe shyness wasn't really such a problem after all? Maybe shyness was, in fact, an essential part of the patient's personality and actually what made her exceptional?

So, what did all this mean to me? I knew I loved to give advice and help others, but I was already doing that. What could I do about it on a bigger, perhaps even global, scale? How could I put my self-confidence, high energy, and waves of creativity to work in this cause? I decided that day in Las Vegas in 2008 that it was time for me to speak out again. I resolved that I would gradually spend less time seeing patients and devote most of my energy to education and advocacy, explaining the myths and stigmas that accompany mental health. Helping people see that the pendulum has swung too far, that not everyone needs therapy or meds, and that embracing who we are is the key to success and happiness.

And that is just what I have done over the last few years.

I increased my media presence and began to appear regularly on the prominent radio and television programs. In early 2009, I launched my website, www.DrDaleArcher.com. It allows me to interact with and offer advice to people who have problems that trouble them but that don't warrant a visit to a psychiatrist. I try to deliver sound advice, based on common sense. I offer hope that the person is not the only one with this type of problem. I seek to give assurance that the issue can be successfully addressed. And of course, in some more serious cases, I can tell the person that the problem really *does* warrant a visit to a psychiatrist. The website has had (and continues to have) an overwhelming response and I feel good that I have been able to help so many folks and do so for free.

But as much as I believed in the value of my media engagements and the website work, I still felt that I could do more. I wanted to present *all* of my ideas in a comprehensive and organized way, to provide a philosophical framework that would help people think broadly and clearly about mental health issues in the context of today's society. And, just as important, I wanted to give people the benefit of my clinical experience by suggesting practical ways for them to approach the problems that they, their family members, and friends and colleagues might be having.

The result is this book. Putting it together has been one of the most challenging and rewarding efforts of my career. It has not only reenergized my commitment to psychiatry, it has opened new opportunities for me to speak up on behalf of a sensible and responsible approach to our collective mental health.

Writing the book has also helped me understand even more about who I am and how to make the most of my own personality profile. I realized that my success at playing poker was, in fact, due to the presence of my dominant traits—*but that it was hardly the best use of them and did not make me truly happy.* Although I didn't have a disorder, they were giving me trouble. But helping patients, bringing ideas to the public, advocating for a better approach to thinking about personality—these activities put my traits to work in a positive way and kept me going with the belief that this is a cause bigger than I am and work that needs to be done.

I hope this book can help you, the reader, come to the same realization that I did. I believe that if you try to conform to what's termed "normal"–by denying your traits or trying to medicate them out of existence–you will lose a source of strength and uniqueness, which is the foundation for your own personal greatness. Truly, *you are who you are*–and you can find great fulfillment in life by understanding your personal character, identifying your traits, and making the most of them.

ONE the eight traits

It's TIME FOR THE introduction of a new order of things in the world of mental health. As a psychiatrist, I feel called to look critically at the overdiagnosing and overmedicating of America. More important, I am driven to spread an empowering new message about mental disorder that places responsibility for identity and mental health back where it belongs—in *your* hands.

I am envisioning a real change in the way we all talk about what it means to be ourselves. I believe that by understanding the eight fundamental behavioral traits and by seeing them as part of a continuum, we can really make a positive change in the way we understand ourselves. By the time you finish this book, I hope you will be able to see that every one of us has *all* of these traits, to some degree, and can analyze where each of our traits falls on a one-to-ten continuum (more on this in a moment). You'll be able to say:

"I'm an eight on the ADHD continuum."

"I am a seven on the narcissism continuum."

"I am a seven on the bipolar continuum."

"I am a two on the OCD continuum."

What's more, you should be able to recognize exactly how your dominant traits have aided you in the past. "I would never have had the desire to do that ten-day solo sailing trip if I wasn't an ADHD eight," you might say, as I do. Or even better: "I have all the strengths I need to go on that trip I've always dreamed of. There's nothing to stop me now."

ATTENTION DEFICIT/HYPERACTIVE CONTINUUM				
PLACID		ADVENTURESOME		ADHD
0	3	5	7	10+
Absent		Dominant		Superdominant

Here's a story for you. It's about me, but it could easily be about you or lots of other people.

One day when I was in fifth grade, my homeroom teacher called in sick and we had a substitute teacher for the day, whom I'll call Ms. J. When this young woman walked into the classroom, I was pretty sure I understood what she was all about.

I decided to see if I was right about her. To do so, I would perform a series of experiments. My first one involved spitballs. I'm not sure if kids still shoot spitballs, so let me give you a quick primer on this technique:

1. Tear off small bit of paper, ideally from homework assignment.
2. Wad up paper, place in mouth, and moisten with saliva (aka spit).
3. Remove paper from mouth and compress into hard little ball.

4. Insert ball into one end of straw, place mouth at other end.

5. Blow hard.

I prepared the first spitball and waited until Ms. J was at the blackboard with her back turned. *Ptooey!* The spitball shot across the room and hit the neck of a kid in the first row. Ms. J faced us. If she noticed the disruption, she didn't let on. Oh my, yes, I was quite right about her.

I followed up on my experiment by sending several rubber bands zinging across the room before upping the ante to a whole new level: paper airplanes.

That did it.

My airplane missed its kid target and nailed Ms. J's right knee-cap. She gasped. She turned red. She looked on the brink of tears. She hastily departed the room and, a moment later, returned with the assistant principal, Mr. B. Without hesitation, he called me to the front of the room and glared at me. "D," he said sternly. (D was my nickname in school.) I slumped a bit. "Yes?" Mr. B spoke in a low, controlled tone. "If you don't behave, I will have to call your parents. I will tell your mother and father that you have been disrupting class and that someone will have to come get you and take you home."

Despite the way this story makes me sound, I was actually a pretty obedient kid. I told Mr. B that I would behave. I apologized to Ms. J. I went back to my desk. Mr. B departed. I leaned my chair up against the wall. Ms. J continued the lesson. I fell asleep.

I feel a little bad when I tell this story. Ms. J was probably a shy woman whose personality type was not particularly well suited to substitute teaching fifth graders. So let me take this opportunity to apologize (again) for ruining her day. Sorry, Ms. J!

My spitball story provides a textbook case of the condition called attention deficit/hyperactivity disorder, or ADHD. Symptoms include inability to focus, acting out, and fidgeting. According to traditional ways of thinking about this disorder, when such symptoms become disruptive—as they did that day in Ms. J's class—they are no longer considered normal personality traits. They become abnormal, signaling a mental disorder that needs to be treated, usually with a combination of therapy and medication, typically a psychostimulant such as Ritalin or Adderall. What's more, anyone who exhibits the symptoms—and goes in for treatment—is labeled mentally ill. They are categorized, stigmatized, and often scarred for life. Good thing for me that my escapade didn't occur recently or I might have been taken to a doc and medicated on the spot!

This is the traditional way of thinking about certain personality traits. My mission is to do whatever it takes to blow that thinking out of the water. And I'll use every tool at my disposal to do so, including, if necessary, spitballs.

The Box Called Normal

Our current way of thinking about personality can be summed up in a single phrase: "the box called normal."

Inside this box we put everybody who seems okay. Once upon a time, the majority of folks fit into this box because *most* of us thought of ourselves as, well, normal.

But here's the problem. The box called normal is getting *smaller* and smaller and smaller every day. It used to be that only those people with very serious conditions and problems—psychosis or severe mood disorders—would be kicked out of the box. They were quietly sent to treatment and preferably forgotten about. No matter how different the rest of us were from each other, we were all crammed in the box together, just being ourselves.

Now, consider these behavioral traits:

Restlessness

Irritability

Difficulty concentrating

Talkativeness

Do any of these traits describe you or someone you know? They certainly apply to me. I have been known to be restless. As a kid, I sometimes had difficulty concentrating. And, as my own kids will tell you, I can definitely be talkative.

Well, any one of these traits could push me (or you) out of the box called normal. The traits are all legitimate diagnostic criteria for serious mental illness, taken right out of the *Diagnostic and Statistical Manual of Mental Disorders,* commonly known as the DSM, the bible of diagnosis, the standard reference for the American psychiatric profession. (The DSM is currently in its fourth edition, with a fifth due out in May of 2013.)

The problem, as I've said, is that these are also "symptoms" that almost everyone has. We all get restless now and again. Everyone gets irritable. Who hasn't had difficulty concentrating? Almost everyone chatters on from time to time. So what's the limit? How irritable do you have to get to be labeled abnormal?

The answer is that the box of normal is getting dangerously small and it's not just the fault of the psychiatrists. Everybody seems to have caught diagnostic fever. Parents, teachers, colleagues, friends, distant relatives—everybody is prepared to make a diagnosis. The child who is bored in school has ADHD. The person who is super well organized has OCD. If you become a little too excited about things you're manic. If your moods shift frequently you're bipolar. If you show healthy self-confidence you're probably a narcissist. The list goes on and on. Such judgments stereotype people, limit them, marginalize them. They don't help us understand ourselves. Rather, we get the feeling that society does not value our highly individualized ways of behaving in certain situations and of coping with life's ups and downs.

We are, somehow, psychologically "off."

In fact, it's reached the point where *26 percent of Americans are considered to have one or more diagnosable mental health disorders.*[1]

The only word for that statistic is "ludicrous." A disorder of any kind is, by definition, something wrong, screwed up, malfunctioning. A *mental* disorder is an irregularity in the functioning of the brain. If the brains of one quarter of the U.S. population are disordered, then something is very, very wrong with the human mind. Or with our society.

But I don't think that's the case. I believe that for the most part, the human brain is perfectly fine. In fact, it's downright amazing. The real problem is the way we think about and diagnose mental illness.

Now, let me be quick to say that I am *not* suggesting that mental illness isn't a real and very serious issue. If you have ever struggled with one of these disorders, or someone close to you has, you know that they can be painful, debilitating, and even life-threatening. As a clinical psychiatrist, I've seen how severe mental health disorders can hurt individuals and their loved ones.

What I am saying is that we need to think differently about how we define these conditions. We have to reframe the conversation and redefine the box called normal.

THE OVERMEDICATED MIND

To do that, we have to understand what causes mental disorders.

We now know that in most cases of major disorders, genetic factors play a role. We also know that severe mental illness typically is caused by a chemical imbalance in the brain. Today we look in particular at the serotonin and dopamine transporter genes as the locations for certain major mental health disorders.

This understanding has been a long time coming. Thirty years ago, as a student of psychiatry, I had reservations about the various types of therapies and counseling that were taught in most psychiatric residencies and medical schools and I resented having to spend time in those classes. Why? Because I believed that we would achieve the optimal state of mental health—for individuals and our society—through a combination of neuroscience and pharmaceutics.

For many years, it looked as if I was right. A series of major pharmaceutical breakthroughs over the past fifty years has really transformed psychiatry. We can now successfully treat disorders including schizophrenia, bipolar disorder, and major depression with medications that alleviate symptoms and improve quality of life for most patients. The pharmaceutical industry has blossomed, some would say ballooned, around the development and production of these drugs.

But I was also wrong. A funny thing happened with all the research that was being funded. We learned that brain chemistry can also be fundamentally affected by *psychotherapy*, not just by meds. The power of positive thinking really works and can help shape our reality. But even though psychotherapy and positive psychology have proved to be every bit as effective as meds for treating some psychiatric conditions, the pendulum keeps swinging farther and farther in the other direction—toward even more diagnoses for more people and even more meds being prescribed.

All of this has contributed to a very clear—and to me disturbing—trend in the pharmaceutical world: Everyone is taking more legally prescribed and over-the-counter drugs, for more reasons, than ever before. Of course, they are not just prescriptions for issues related to mental health. There are the painkillers. Sleeping aids. Cold medicine. Cough medicine. Cough and cold medicine combined. Contraceptives. Antidotes for erectile dysfunction. Migraine relievers. Remedies for heart disease. Medications to reduce risk of heart disease. Asthma steroids. Weight-loss potions. Heartburn tablets and liquids and gel caps. Antidepressants. Psychostimulants.

Today, 47 percent of American adults report having taken at least one prescription drug in the last month, and 20 percent of children (that's one in five!) have done so.[2] As Americans, we suffer through all kinds of side effects of these drugs—some of them are almost as bad as the condition we're trying to relieve—and we pay extraordinary amounts of money to look and feel as though we are just like everyone else. In 2007, Americans spent $25 billion on antidepressants and antipsychotics alone.[3] That same year, 3.9 million people (that's one in seventy-six) received Social Security disability payments because they had some kind of problem with a mental illness.[4] The cost of medicating our minds is truly mind-blowing.

Why is this happening? It's a complex issue and there are many factors involved (including certain insurance companies that won't pay psychiatrists to do therapy), but one that I know about firsthand is the current state of the psychiatric industry. Psychiatrists, aware that their profession is not considered to be a "real" or "hard" science (that is, one based on laboratory tests, biopsies, or imaging studies) have put less emphasis on the traditional talking cure, the results of which are less easy to evaluate, and turned increasingly to medications, because they are so tangible and the results they deliver are easier to quantify. And also, of course, because they truly do help many, many people.

This reliance on medications has further encouraged the pharmaceutical companies, which see an ever-expanding market for their products. The pharma companies form various kinds of relationships with psychiatrists and research scientists to help them formulate, develop, test, and evaluate the effectiveness of their drugs. The flow of money and authority from the drug makers into the scientific and psychiatric community has served to build the ubiquity and importance of medications even more, and not always in a good way. In 2003, a study found that when a pharmaceutical company funds a drug trial, there is a better chance that the trial will show that the drug is effective for its intended purpose than if the drug company has *not* funded the trial.[5] In other words, a study is more likely to make a drug look good if it's paid for by the company that sells the drug.

No great surprise there, but what *was* surprising to me is that until that study was released, drugs were approved by the FDA on the basis of trials that had been managed by—get this—the drug companies. That's no longer the case, but the trials are still not completely trustworthy and the relationships between big pharma and the scientific community are not completely clean. As a researcher/scientist friend told me, if a drug company funds one of his trials and the results aren't in line with what the company expects, there's a good chance he won't be running the next trial for them. That puts a lot of pressure on researchers to get the results the company wants.

Once again, let me say: *I am not against medications.* I have seen them do too much good to suggest that we should halt drug trials or stop looking for the best medications to treat the mental disorders that plague us. However, I believe that medications should be just one piece of the puzzle of health care and, as often as possible, the last one we put in place. I am not alone in this belief. There is a growing consensus among physicians who want to move away from medications to treat certain physical conditions and toward more fundamental changes in lifestyle. If a primary-care physician finds that her patient has high blood pressure, she may not immediately prescribe medication. Instead, she may encourage the patient to make changes in diet, exercise more, get more sleep, or find ways to eliminate or lessen the factors that cause stress in the patient's life. Only after these methods have been tried and have not achieved the desired results will the physician suggest a medication that could help.

The approach that works for high blood pressure and other bodily ailments can also be applied to the treatment of mental health. When a patient describes symptoms or behavioral characteristics that are not obvious manifestations of severe mental disorders, hold the medication! The doctor—whether pediatrician, family doctor, or psychiatrist—should first see if the complaints can be alleviated in some other way.

Even more important—and this is fundamental to the concept of this book—the "patient" (who may not really be a patient at all) should be encouraged to look at his or her personality traits in the new way that I have described. People must be helped to see that they can embrace the things that make them seem different. What's more, we can completely change the way we think about our personality profile. Rather than see your dominant trait as abnormal, you can come to think of it as self-defining, unique, and special to you. The characteristic that sometimes seems like a burden or an obstacle may in fact be your greatest asset. What you thought of as a weakness may be a strength. What seemed like a barrier may be your path to greater success and happiness than you have ever known.

That sounds like I'm overreaching, I know. But bear with me. Not only do I believe it's true, I've seen it play out with hundreds of patients and friends, relatives and colleagues.

This idea has roots in evolutionary theory. The group theory of evolution, which has received increasing interest in recent years, suggests that because humans live in interdependent groups, evolution has favored the kind of personality *specialization* that we're talking about. When one person is particularly adventurous, for example, or especially well organized, or an exceptionally charismatic leader, everyone else in the group benefits. But when we seek out diagnoses and medications so that we can stuff everyone back into the box called normal, we stifle the full range of human diversity. As individuals, our potential for personal satisfaction decreases. As a group—as a society—we suffer.

The Traits on a Continuum

I believe there are eight important personality traits that when extremely dominant can constitute a disorder. Almost everybody on earth exhibits at least one of these traits to some degree.

The traits are usually no secret. Most people are quite astute judges of character (at least, of *other* people's character!) and know very well that Ms. J is shy and that Mr. B is pretty self-confident and that the kid in the back of the room shooting spitballs is a little bit hyper and easily bored. These traits can be seen as positive and powerful, or as problematic and limiting, or, most often, as *somewhere in between.* More on that in a second.

The eight fundamental traits of human behavior are also well known within the psychiatric community. In the *Diagnostic and Statistical Manual of Mental Disorders* they are all classified as (just as the title would make you suspect) mental disorders— conditions such as bipolar disorder, ADHD, OCD, or narcissistic personality disorder. These terms are not only clearly defined in the lexicon of psychiatry, they have also passed into general, popular usage.

In recent years, the psychiatric community has begun to look at these traits (aka disorders) in a more nuanced way—a way that should someday start to expand the normal box—by placing them along a continuum or spectrum. At one end of the continuum, the personality trait may not appear at all. It is what I call *absent* (e.g., you are not shy). At the other end, the trait is so pronounced that it almost completely defines who you are and makes it difficult for you to function. I call that *superdominant* (you are so shy you don't want to leave your house—social anxiety disorder). Then there are many degrees of the trait in between those two extremes. That is, the trait is present to the point of being *dominant,* but not overpoweringly so. (You are a very self-contained person with great inner strength who does not need or want a tremendous amount of social interaction to be successful, happy, and productive.)

I believe that the continuum model is the right direction for us to go, and it's the best way for us to expand the box and to free ourselves from this spiral of overdiagnosis and overmedication. We need to see that a large number of us have these traits in varying degrees. We have to stop seeing them as negatives. We have to recognize the positive aspects of each trait. And we have to get better at understanding when and how each trait can become superdominant and thus a problem—for the person and for society—and how to manage it.

Before we talk about the traits in more detail, let me explain how I arrived at these eight in particular, and why there are eight and not ten or twenty. First, all eight traits line up with well-known psychiatric disorders. I see many of the other, lesser-known disorders as subcategories of these eight traits. For example, borderline personality disorder shares symptoms with both bipolar disorder and histrionic personality disorder. Second, I wanted to focus on traits for which research has been conducted (and is still being pursued) into genetic links about causation—that is, why, over the millennia, these traits have become so dominant and persistent and prevalent in human society. Given these two criteria, I choose not to include certain types of behaviors, such as passive-aggressiveness, because they do not really define personality.

In addition, and just as important, I have found in my own practice that these eight traits are the most prevalent ones that manifest themselves along a continuum and that people worry most about. I see plenty of depression as well, but I consider that to fall within the anxiety continuum. For all these traits, though, when folks reach a nine or ten on the continuum, it's very common to also experience associated depression. In fact, depression can often be the presenting complaint, which is why it's referred to as "the common cold of psychiatry." As a doctor, my job is to assess the underlying traits that may be a part of the problem and address the situation in its entirety. And plenty of people come to me with problems related to drug abuse and addiction, which I see as a disease rather than as a personality trait.

Now, let's talk about the traits in more detail.

Be prepared, because when you see the *clinical* definitions you will likely say, "That's not me." Or, "There can be nothing good about *that.*" So I'm going to list them as the positive first, when the trait is present and even ascendant, and then show the DSM classification—when it is *superdominant*—second. Later, I've also provided some examples of real people—someone I know, a patient, or a famous person—for each trait.

Adventurous (ADHD)

When this trait is dominant, but not superdominant, you are easily bored with routine, can be bold, ignore danger, and take calculated risks. When it is superdominant, it can be diagnosed as *attention deficit/hyperactivity disorder* or ADHD. You find it hard to sit still, slow down, focus, reflect, or act in a measured, deliberate way.

Perfectionist (OCD)

You notice and care about details that most of us would overlook. When the trait is ascendant, you're a perfectionist with an eagle eye for the important specifics. When the trait is superdominant, we might diagnose it as *obsessive-compulsive disorder,* or OCD. You simply can't get away from the details. You create obsessive and inflexible routines for yourself. You can't control certain actions.

Shy (SOCIAL ANXIETY DISORDER)

As a shy person, you have a lot going on inside. You can live and work alone, or with close friends and family only, very happily and comfortably. If the trait is superdominant, you have *social anxiety disorder.* This disorder can create problems at work, school, and in other social situations.

Hyper-alert (GENERALIZED ANXIETY DISORDER)

If you have this trait you may often be incredibly alert, but you are focused on real problems and you use your attention as a motivating force. You plan for the worst and prepare accordingly. Your anxiety serves as an early warning system to bring up details that need to be addressed. When this trait is superdominant, the diagnosis is *generalized anxiety disorder,* which is fear without a valid reason or cause. You rush from task to task, are never content, and worry incessantly over everything.

Dramatic (HISTRIONIC)

You are full of emotion and display it fully, unashamedly, and genuinely. You feel deeply about things and show emotion appropriately, often when others are afraid to. When this trait is superdominant, we say that you have *histrionic personality disorder.* Everything is a drama, no matter how big or small it might be. Emotion always outweighs rationality.

Self-Focused (NARCISSISTIC)

You're proud of who and what you are. You exude confidence and trust your skills and intuition. People are drawn to you. They want to be around you and follow you. When this trait is superdominant it becomes pathological narcissism with a diagnosis of *narcissis-tic personality disorder.* You are self-focused to the point of exclud-ing, or being unaware, of others. It's all about *you* and what you want and you don't care much, if at all, about other people.

High Energy (BIPOLAR)

You live life at top speed, commit fully, go nonstop, pour every ounce of yourself into what you do, can be tremendously creative and productive. This dynamic energy, when superdominant, can be called *bipolar*–your behavior becomes manic and out of control. After a while you may crash and go into a full-on funk that can be-come a severe depression.

Magical (SCHIZOPHRENIA)

You are highly intuitive. You sense things. You take action on beliefs and insights that cannot necessarily be quantified. You may have a vision of the way things could be. You have faith. When the trait is superdominant it can become *schizophrenia.* You hear voices and see things that aren't there. You live in a world of unreality.

MAKING THE MOST OF A DOMINANT TRAIT

Does this make sense to you? Or do you think I'm sugarcoating some very serious problems? Maybe you think, "Dale says that being self-focused can be a good thing, but he's really just talking about a completely self-absorbed narcissist that I could not stand being around."

If that's how you're thinking, try to rein in your skepticism for a little longer. My purpose here is to break down the stigma surrounding labels such as ADHD and bipolar. While I'm totally comfortable saying, "Yeah, I'm a little bit ADHD," I know very well that some folks have a difficult time making a distinction between *adventurous* and *overactive,* especially when it comes to their kids.

But we must learn to make these distinctions. That's the only way to improve our own self-awareness so that we can realize our potential most fully. And it's the best way to better appreciate the traits of others so that we can live and work with them most successfully.

Ultimately, I hope that we will be able to see our dominant traits as some of our best qualities, rather than as liabilities. There is no question, for example, that I have a dominant adventurous trait— I'm an eight on the ADHD continuum. When I was a kid, it got me in all sorts of trouble, even though we didn't have the ADHD diagnosis back then. As an adult, however, this trait has always been an asset. If you were to spend time with me, you would know that I am constantly multitasking: juggling meetings, phone calls, emails, events, travel, writing, speaking, social engagements, and family obligations. The ability to do so is essential for anyone who works with the news media. And the love of adventure allowed me to start a whole new career in middle age.

Being adventurous, like all the behavioral traits, isn't always an easy trait to have, precisely because it works on a continuum *in time,* too. In other words, in some periods of my life the adventurous trait is nicely dominant and takes me into exciting new endeavors. (Poker playing, for example.) At other times, it verges on superdominance and gets closer to ADHD. (Restlessness with my psychiatric practice, too *much* focus on poker playing, and constant pursuit of new extreme sports to participate in.)

But over the years I have become extremely aware of my traits and how they appear at different places on the continuum. So today I have structured my life around my adventurous nature. As much as possible, my work, relationships, and outside activities are all in tune with who I truly am.

And it's not just me. Look around you and you'll find endless examples of people with very pronounced personality traits—strong but not superdominant—who have achieved all kinds of wonderful things, big and small. Let me give you a few examples:

David Neeleman is the founder of JetBlue, the highly successful airline. David's story is well known. He fidgeted through his school years and was diagnosed with ADHD when he was an adult. Along the way, David found a way to channel his spirit into a world-class achievement. He has even said that he wouldn't have it any other way.

Like David, people with superdominant ADHD may be almost unable to succeed in a job or career that doesn't totally engage them in every way. They have to do something they can immerse themselves in, genuinely love, and focus on relentlessly. If they can find that work, they can become top performers.

Mardi is a salesperson who makes major presentations to big customers all the time. She goes over and over the presentation in advance, thinks about all the angles, tries to anticipate questions and develop answers, investigates the customer and the competition. She hates to fail. Can't stand to lose the sale. She definitely worries and feels anxiety about her work, and you may describe her as high strung. But her anxiety drives her to do her best. She has taken meds in the past, but felt she totally lost her edge and so she stopped taking them. Anxiety at the middle of the continuum is a part of daily life and normal in many everyday contexts: coping with new situations, adjusting to new people, responding to dangers. It can sharpen the senses, preparing us for action while enhancing our learning and problem-solving skills.

Take a look at *Melinda.* When Melinda was a child, she preferred to read books or take walks by herself rather than play with the neighborhood kids. Over the years, her family diagnosed her as shy. But her shyness only becomes superdominant in certain kinds of situations, like parties and large social events, especially ones where she doesn't know many people.

Now Melinda avoids going to big parties that make her feel uncomfortable, rather than taking a medication that could help her get through the events. She knows that she's shy and something of a loner, but she also has an independent mind and spirit. She prefers to work outside the spotlight, and she has found a perfect situation for her personality: working at a large family-owned chain restaurant as a menu developer. She can work at home and she interacts—often by email or on the phone—with family members when she needs to. She has one very close friend.

Melinda has created menus that have proved so successful and popular that the restaurant's business has increased by 75 percent. Society might say that Melinda has social anxiety. I say she is *being true to herself*—making the most of her traits and loving it.

How would you "diagnose" *Julia*? She is always very put together with neatly coiffed hair and sharp clothing. She is obviously very self-confident. She performs brilliantly, takes considered risks, and is good at articulating goals and objectives. Julia can mobilize people to do their best and is not overly bothered by criticism or set back by negative turns of events. She can persuade people to join a cause. She proceeds boldly under pressure. No wonder she was chosen to lead a major fund drive by United Way. Is Julia narcissistic? Yes, a bit, but in a positive way. Pathologically narcissistic? Definitely not. Pathological narcissists typically overestimate their talents and exaggerate their accomplishments. They think of themselves as superior to others and, most important, don't care about anyone other than themselves. The self-focused person is often highly charismatic and a real leader who is realistic about how good she is, because she *is* good.

Jill is a larger-than-life person. She likes to entertain people.

She tells wonderful stories and genuinely funny jokes and, above all, has a wonderful singing voice. Unfortunately for her, Jill earned her degree in business and then went to work for a high-profile company with a fast-track job. The work did not please her. Too rigid. Not enough expression. She described her misery to her friends and fellow workers with great passion. Sometimes they listened. Sometimes they wanted her just to shut up.

In the evenings, however, Jill came alive. The negative feelings that came from her work were replaced by a wonderful ability to express emotion and tell stories through song. She sang with various groups and loved every minute of it. At last, Jill—and everybody else at the company—came to the realization that she was seriously in the wrong line of work. One day her boss said as much to her. On the spot, Jill said, "You're right. I quit!" She said good-bye to a $250,000 annual salary and set her sights on a career as a singer.

"It was the hardest thing I ever did," Jill told me. But she knew she had to find a place where it would be okay, even expected and valued, to be *dramatic.* She lived on her savings while she built a singing career. Now she has released her first CD and landed a number of performing gigs. Jill tapped in to one of the main strengths of this trait and created a whole new and exciting career around her inborn gifts.

Courtney is a creative executive at a small advertising agency based in New York. She goes through phases of incredible creativity when she seems to be bursting with breakthrough new ideas and surprising solutions to difficult client problems. She dives into projects that she feels passionate about and works long, hard hours to complete them successfully. She works late into the evening and on weekends, and her enthusiasm and optimism seem boundless.

Occasionally, however, when Courtney has been working for a long stretch of time at full strength, she will have a dip. Usually it's just a matter of needing a weekend of downtime. She'll stay in her apartment, order food in, watch movies, read, and ignore her email. By Monday, she's ready to go again. Sometimes, although rarely, the downtime borders on depression. She feels sad, a bit down, with low energy. But the mood never lasts for long and she chooses to think of it as recharging her batteries.

If her high energy included full-on severe mood swings and prevented her from satisfying her clients or keeping her job, you might say that Courtney was bipolar. The superdominant bipolar person has dramatic mood shifts, from extremely manic to utterly depressed. Courtney is mostly high energy and works in a job where that intensity is put to good use.

Matt, a twenty-year-old star center on his university's basketball team, will do anything to give his team an edge, including wearing his "lucky socks." He wears the same socks as long as his team is winning (and it usually does). His thinking is *magical* in nature.

New research demonstrates that magical thinking—the leap of faith from needing proof to believing in something beyond what we know to be true—is far more common than people acknowledge. The quality of magical thinking begins with faith in a pair of lucky socks, but it can also include intuition, empathy, and the belief in things that cannot be proved. At the extreme, magical thinkers can lose their sense of reality altogether, a state that psychiatrists refer to as psychosis. But without a little bit of magical thinking, most of us would have a hard time doing anything at all. And perhaps more important, it is often magical thinking that allows us to find meaning in life.

Over to You

My purpose here is to encourage you to get in touch with your own behavioral traits. I want to help you realize that whether you have been diagnosed with a mental disorder or not, you are who you are—and that's a good thing.

This book features one chapter for each of the eight traits. They are loaded with information about each trait's ascendant strengths, true stories about people I know who have built their lives around their traits, and advice on everything from career planning to relationships.

At the end of the book is a series of questionnaires, one for each trait. The questionnaires were developed in my clinic in Louisiana with the help of my colleague, psychologist Dr. Jerry Whiteman. They are designed to help you understand your personality profile, which traits are dominant, and which traits are superdominant. I advise you to go to the back of the book and take the tests now, before you read about the eight traits. Then you'll be able to read the chapters with your own personal profile in mind. As you go through the questionnaires, please note that the continuums run from zero to ten-plus. If you are a ten-plus for your trait, that means you have an extremely strong personality trait in this area, but it does *not* automatically mean that you need meds or a diagnosis. Jerry and I both know some "ten-plus" people who have learned to live with a superdominant trait.

The eight key traits contribute in powerful, important ways to your psychological profile. They are what makes you distinct and different from everybody else on earth. They affect how you think and behave, and what you feel. That profile may shift over time as your circumstances change or as you put your energies into different things at different stages of your life. These traits do not carve out boundaries for you or box you into a rigid identity—that's the last thing I'd want to suggest. Rather, I hope that as you come to understand these key traits and learn which ones affect you the most, you'll see that they also bestow upon you unique, special strengths. I firmly believe that when you build your life around these strengths, they will rise to the surface and guide your life in positive ways.

So let's start out with my "favorite" trait, the one that has been mostly a boon to me in my own life, although sometimes a problem, and the one that gets so much attention (and medication) these days: *Adventurous* ADHD.

TWO adventurous ADHD

WHEN MY COLLEAGUE'S SON Seth was in his senior year of college, he set out to establish a successful career. Along with his peers, he wrote cover letters and sent his résumé to dozens of major banks and corporations around the country.

Several big businesses responded, and in the fall of 2008, Seth found himself in an interview at Bloomberg, the information provider, in New York City. For many aspiring young people, it was the perfect opportunity: a sales position at a major corporation with huge potential for upward mobility. But, Seth told me, he blew the interview.

"I knew after the interview that I did not get the job. It was just a bad conversation," Seth recalled.

That gloomy Friday afternoon, Seth flew back to school. "I remember that I was quite upset. I stared out the window of the plane and I could see my distorted reflection in the plastic. Something clicked inside me. I realized I don't feel comfortable in a suit. I don't belong on an airplane flying back and forth between New York and Washington." Seth looked around at the other people on the flight. "Everybody was dressed exactly like I was. They all looked somber.

For a split second, I felt like I was one of them." The feeling was not one of comfort and belonging. Quite the opposite. "I told myself I don't want to be like everybody else. I'm done with this. I'm going to follow my dream. I want to be on the other side of the world."

In the following months, Seth thought carefully about his future and his personality. He is an active person, always seeking out the next thing, always multitasking, always looking for adventures. "I constantly need something new," Seth said.

There is no doubt that Seth is someone with an adventurous personality—an eight on the ADHD continuum.

THE CONTINUUM MODEL: ADVENTUROUS

ATTENTION DEFICIT/HYPERACTIVE CONTINUUM				
PLACID		ADVENTURESOME		ADHD
0	3	5	7	10+
Absent		Dominant		Superdominant

Growing up, almost everyone knew at least one child with an adventurous spirit. It's that boy who sat in the back of the classroom, shooting airplanes across the room. (Yes, I mean me!) The girl who fidgeted endlessly and was never able to sit calmly in her chair. The kid who always forgot to bring his homework to school, or forgot to do his homework, or never seemed to hear what the teacher was saying.

I'm thinking about kids who are like Calvin from the comic strip *Calvin and Hobbes,* who seems to spend most of his class time in outer space, in the future, or in the Jurassic era. Or like Mark Twain's hero Huckleberry Finn, who was forced to study spelling for an hour every day. "I couldn't stand it much longer," Huck says. "It was deadly dull, and I was fidgety." In the book, his teacher, Miss Watson, threatens him with eternal damnation in "the bad place" if he doesn't pay attention. This does not seem like such a bad alternative to Huck. "I said I wished I was there," Huck admits. "But I didn't mean no harm. All I wanted was to go somewheres; all I wanted was a change, I warn't particular."[1]

Sounds a lot like Seth, a hundred years earlier.

Many famous people have been associated with this trait. Historical speculations have included figures such as Andrew Carnegie, Christopher Columbus, Thomas Edison, Agatha Christie, and Pablo Picasso. Some modern-day superstars could also be seen as ranking high on the ADHD continuum, such as Olympic swimmer Michael Phelps, performers Justin Timberlake and Whoopi Goldberg, and superstar basketball player Michael Jordan.

These people are passionate, curious, and energetic. They are great multitaskers and extraordinary explorers. They excel in times of challenge—war, an expedition, perhaps the Olympic Games. Throughout history, they have been selected for their extraordinary achievements—and we love them for it.

All of these people fall somewhere on the higher end of the ADHD continuum. People on the low end of the scale tend to be calm, placid, and focused; as you move up the scale, you become increasingly adventurous and energetic until eventually—if the right conflux of genetics, environment, and context occurs—your trait can become superdominant and often debilitating. At this point, the adventurous personality slips into the realm of diagnosable ADHD.

But at its best, being adventurous can be a great strength. After his airplane epiphany, Seth came to the conclusion that the corporate life wasn't for him. So as his friends sent their résumés to bank after bank and consultancy after consultancy, he applied for positions teaching English abroad. After graduating from college, he caught the first flight to Moscow to teach—and, to the amazement of his friends and family, he hasn't looked back. His goal: to visit every country in the world.

But you don't have to be a world traveler to live an adventurous life. In this chapter, I'll look at the origins of ADHD and I'll talk about the ADHD continuum. I'll describe some of the ways to cope with the challenges of being—or living with—someone with an adventurous spirit. And I'll describe how some adventurous folks have harnessed their strengths to do amazing things—from sixteenth-century explorers to rock stars, pilots, and social media entrepreneurs.

REDEFINING THE DEFICIT IN ATTENTION DEFICIT

To understand what it means to have an *adventurous spirit,* we need to take a close look at the way people think about attention deficit/hyperactivity disorder (ADHD).

ADHD is typically divided into two types: inattentive or hyperactive. ADD is diagnosed from a list of symptoms including failure to give attention to details, difficulty sustaining attention, and not listening when spoken to. If you have at least six of the relevant symptoms, then you may be diagnosed with ADD. If you also exhibit symptoms of hyperactivity—like fidgeting, talking excessively, or having difficulty waiting—then you may receive a diagnosis of ADHD. In this book, I have chosen to use ADHD as a general term to refer to folks with adventurous personalities, whether or not they are also hyperactive.

ADHD is traditionally thought of as a childhood disorder, more or less limited to those under the legal drinking age. But new theories have led to the creation of a third category, adult ADHD, which can affect you throughout your life.

If you've never seen the diagnostic criteria for ADHD before, you may be thinking: "Gee, those are pretty vague guidelines." You may even think, "It seems like all the children I know fit those criteria, at least some of the time. Does everyone have ADHD?"

The answer is, of course not. In fact, being adventurous only becomes a problem in a very small number of individuals. Many more people have personalities that are not suited to classroom learning. Some of us are visual learners. Some of us are active learners. Sitting in one place and studying a single subject for hours at a stretch does not work for everyone.

My young friend Seth spoke about this very problem. "In those early years," he told me, "I wanted to be outside. I just wanted to be doing anything other than sitting inside all day long."

Seth's grades suffered when he was in elementary school because he couldn't get his homework done, and he had difficulty focusing in class. "The teacher would say, 'Okay, let's sit down and do this assignment,'" Seth recalled. "I'd have no problem doing it for ten minutes. But after that I wanted to do something else. Even if it was to switch to a class like math. I just wanted to keep it interesting."

It can be frustrating when your child's personality makes it difficult for him or her to learn well at school. So when it was discovered that psychostimulant medications such as Adderall or Ritalin can help people apply excess energy to a specific subject, like a homework assignment, it's no surprise that many parents jumped at the opportunity. In fact, Seth's mom and dad told me they considered a psychostimulant for him, but ultimately decided against it.

That's why when the DSM first defined diagnostic criteria for ADHD, it was a godsend. Creating a definition for ADHD allowed parents to understand that their child wasn't simply unintelligent or a disordered thinker—he had a chemical imbalance of the brain that made it difficult for him to function in our society, or at least in certain parts of our society, notably our schools.

As I've said before: *I am not rejecting the diagnosis and medi-*

cal treatment of attention deficit/hyperactivity disorder. In the last ten years, however, ADHD diagnoses have increased to the point of absurdity. In 2008, five million children (8 percent of the total population of kids between the ages of three and seventeen) were diagnosed as having ADHD. If you look only at boys, the percentage was 11 percent.[2] (Yes, ADHD is dramatically more common among boys.) This increase is something to be taken seriously, because the ADHD diagnosis can be stigmatizing, making a child feel bad about himself, and putting him outside the box of normal for life.

Further, ADHD meds can have negative side effects. Adderall and Ritalin are central nervous system stimulants that are in the same class of drugs as cocaine. They can be powerfully addictive, especially when used as quick fixes to get focused. A segment on *60 Minutes* reported that more than 50 percent of college juniors and seniors—and about 80 percent of juniors and seniors in fraternities and sororities—take Adderall to study and perform better. It's become a dangerous and quite common practice.[3]

So what's causing this overdiagnosis and overmedication? It's not because there are really more kids with the superdominant trait. And it's not because diagnostic tools are improving so that previously undiagnosed cases are showing up. To understand why this increase occurred, I'd like to turn to Allen Frances, the lead editor of the *Diagnostic and Statistical Manual of Mental Disorders-IV,* the most recent edition of psychiatry's diagnostic bible. In an interview with Gary Greenberg in *Wired* magazine in January 2011, Frances blamed the DSM-IV itself. "We made mistakes that had terrible consequences," Frances is quoted as saying. One of these consequences, the article notes, is that diagnoses of ADHD have skyrocketed. Greenberg writes: "Frances thinks his manual inadvertently facilitated these epidemics—and, in the bargain, fostered an increasing tendency to chalk up life's difficulties to mental illness and then treat them with psychiatric drugs."

Sounds exactly like something I might say!

So how do we solve this problem? One thought is that we should tighten up the diagnostic criteria. If they were more specific and objective, it would be more difficult for a child who is on the middle of the continuum—adventurous—to be misdiagnosed with ADHD. This is, I think, the guiding principle for the new DSM-V, due to be released in May 2013. But this is just a modification, not a solution. The better answer is that instead of trying to move the line that the DSM theoretically draws in the sand between those of us who are normal and those of us who are not, we need to erase that line altogether.

Not Every Kid Is Wired the Same Way

I recognize that true ADHD is not easy for anyone, neither for the children who must try to understand and live with it, nor for the parents who must help them, nor, for that matter, the teachers and others who interact with both kids and parents.

I remember the story of the Wilson family, whose seven-year-old son, Dwight, was taking medication for ADHD. (They contacted me through my website. I have changed their names.) One day Dwight came home from school very upset. His mother, Barbara, asked him if something had happened. Dwight didn't want to talk about it. Finally, she got him to tell the story. One of the other children had started getting on his case and finally called Dwight "retarded." Despite his diagnosis and the side effects of the medication, Dwight had been a basically happy child, but the incident had a profound effect on him. He became withdrawn and, at times, troubled. The change was heartbreaking for everyone who knew him, especially, of course, his parents.

Although Dwight had tried several different medications for his condition, none of them worked very well. "All the medications he has been on either didn't work at all, made him a zombie, worked for a short time, made him overly emotional, made him not eat, or caused different tics," his mom said. "I'm also worried about his anger. He often yells and throws things at his sister. He is so hyperactive that he has a very hard time doing his homework. It usually takes up to six hours, with lots of yelling and fighting. He used to try hard to learn, but now he couldn't care less."

I urged Barbara to work with her family's child psychiatrist to find a better medication or combination of medications that could really work for Dwight. Every med has its advantages and disadvantages; it all depends on the individual. Often there's one certain drug that can work and make all the difference in the world, but sometimes you need to try many others to finally figure this out. Obviously, the Wilsons hadn't found the right one for Dwight. Rather than give up, I urged Dwight's mom to keep on trying.

Just as important, Dwight needed to view himself from a more positive perspective, to think of himself as an adventurous guy who had a lot of good things going for him, rather than as a sick kid whom people thought of as "retarded." To do that, he would need to work with his teachers to develop some strategies that would let him see how his adventurous nature could work to his advantage. Rather than medicate Dwight into complacency, why not put his energy to work? He could run errands for the teacher, help with end-of-the-day cleanup, and bring balls in from the playground.

Dwight's teachers could also tap in to his love of exploring and trying new things. Why not devise some experiments for him? Expose him to active pursuits, like music or dance? Because Dwight was obviously a very, very bright kid, he could also be encouraged to help other students with academics. This would let him expend more of his excessive energy, while building his self-esteem and proving, beyond a shadow of a doubt, that he was no "retard." In addition, his parents could buy some books about true-life adventurers and explorers and read them to Dwight, to let him see that his adventurous spirit has a place in the world.

I have seen these approaches work for many kids like Dwight, if the teachers and parents are open to and cooperative about putting them into practice. By using their strengths in new ways, such kids can emerge from their shells and become much happier and better adjusted. It will take some perseverance on the part of the parents. They may have to work with their doctor to find the optimal combination and doses of medicines. Eventually, however, I have seen that the new attitude and different approach to activity can take hold. As time goes on, they are often able to lower the dose of meds, and even discontinue them altogether.

One of the most important things that the parents can do in the early years is to help their child establish a self-awareness and self-confidence that he can continue to draw on as he grows up. What happens when a child develops these traits early in life? For the answer we can look at Seth, the adventurous traveler. When he was a kid, Seth was a lot like Dwight—unfocused, distracted, and in trouble at school. But by the time he reached high school, Seth had actually begun to excel in his schoolwork and sports, and especially in friendships with classmates. He was able to achieve a straight-A average in college by adapting his study methods to fit his personality. "When I studied for exams," he explained, "I would have the TV on and be emailing or texting my friends. Sometimes I'd also be talking on the phone and writing an essay at the same time." When he was a kid, such study habits would have been forbidden by his parents. Out of the best of intentions, they would try to make him do two hours of homework every night. He would sit at his desk, staring at his papers, thinking how boring it all was. In college, he kept his studies interesting and active through his amazing ability to multitask.

This strategy runs counter to the traditional thinking about study habits, but actually, many children and adults learn better this way. In a classic study from 1978, psychologists found that college students who studied in several different, cluttered rooms performed better than those who studied in one single, quiet location.

In a more recent study, scientists discovered that students who learn multiple things simultaneously remember what they learned better than those who study one thing at a time. So we can conclude that many people, like Dwight and Seth, benefit when they mix things up.[4]

And it's critical to get active! Adventurous spirits suffer from excess energy and enthusiasm. When that energy is given a direction, it can propel them to greatness. That's why some athletes have this trait: They take all that energy and use it to become the best basketball player, skier, or dancer they can be. If your child is athletically minded, supporting her interest in organized sports can be a great way to give her direction, help her self-confidence, and use up some of that energy that becomes so distracting during the school day.

These children also benefit from unstructured adventure. Unleashing the creativity of adventurous kids means giving their imagination space to roam. Free play can be physically and mentally stimulating. It can also get their creative juices flowing—a skill that will benefit these kids later in life.

In particular, give your child a chance to play outside. Study after study has revealed that (not at all surprisingly) outdoor play is good for *all* children. It stimulates the senses, engages creative thought processes, helps children understand the natural environment, and improves self-confidence. Outdoor play is especially good for adventurous spirits. When I was a kid, I loved the Boy Scouts. Even though it was a structured setting, I was never bored. Seth told me the same thing—he loves activities that get him outside. In my experience (both clinical and personal), I have found that although kids with ADHD have trouble with many things, such as focusing on certain kinds of rote tasks, the condition also brings with it advantages. For example, these kids can be very good in one-on-one situations, and they are highly aware of their surroundings and able to notice details better than other children.

With these simple sorts of cost-free adjustments, we can harness our children's strengths and achieve tremendous positive results!

An Evolutionary Imperative

To go even further to the root of the adventurous trait, we need to take a look at its evolutionary history. Looking at the way that it has been passed down through the generations leaves us with a bit of a paradox. (We'll touch on this same problem, known in the scientific literature as the "schizophrenia paradox," in several other chapters.)

ADHD has a high percentage of heritability, meaning that if a man with ADHD has four children, three of them will probably show ADHD symptoms.[5] It almost always appears in childhood, which means that it is well established by the time we reach reproductive age. If ADHD was really a bad thing, natural selection should have weeded it out millennia ago.

Why, instead, has this trait survived through the generations? And why, in fact, has it seemingly *flourished?* Or as Thom Hartmann asked in his book *The Edison Gene,* "Is it possible that what we now call a genetic 'disorder' is actually *the* positive adaptation—that 'fortuitous mutation'—that led to the creation of human culture and modern civilization as we know it?"

I don't know if the genes associated with ADHD led, in fact, to the dawn of civilization. But evidence suggests that the traits that we associate with ADHD have historically given their bearers an evolutionary advantage. That's why scientists refer to the long allele of the dopamine transporter gene—the gene linked with ADHD—as "the explorer gene."

What do they mean by "explorer gene"? In 1999, scientists at the University of California at Irvine studied the genetic makeup of 2,320 individuals from thirty-nine different populations across the globe—groups like the Cheyenne tribe of North America, the Han of China, the Ashkenazi Jews from Eastern Europe, and the Mbuti from Africa. They then looked at the migratory patterns of these groups' ancestors in prehistoric times. They found that people who had a history of long migrations had a larger proportion of long alleles of the dopamine D4 receptor—genetic material associated with novelty-seeking personality, hyperactivity, and risk-taking behaviors.[6]

Why do migratory groups tend to have this gene? The authors concluded that it was most likely because the gene offers some kind of benefit for the people in those groups. All of the traits associated with this gene, they pointed out, are also associated with exploration. "It can be argued reasonably that exploratory behaviors are adaptive in migratory societies because they allowed for more successful exploitation of resources in the particular environment migration entails—usually harsh, frequently challenging, and always providing a multitude of novel stimuli and ongoing challenges to survival."[7]

For millennia, migratory societies benefited from people who were adventurous. But then something happened. In a very short period of time (on the scale of human history) those migratory societies began to farm, and the hunter-gatherer lifestyle was left behind. They settled down and built roads and cities. They invented the wheel—and the cubicle. They stopped being migratory and became sedentary. And the exploratory gene was less in demand.

So is there still a place for adventurous people in today's society?

Ascendant Strengths

Having an adventurous spirit is a real advantage; it confers upon you the following ascendant strengths:

ENERGY High energy levels mean you can accomplish many things in a short amount of time. You might be able to do much more than many people do their entire lives—finish an advanced degree in half the usual time or run a string of successful businesses at once, for example.

PLAYFULNESS You might be a prankster, a jokester, and a trickster—all in good fun, of course. Your fun-loving behavior can give you the power to bring joy, laughter, and smiles to yourself and to others.

ADVENTUROUS SPIRIT You're always seeking new and awakening experiences. You tend to explore, question, or challenge the status quo. And you typically live life without needless worry that you're too old or too worn out to learn something new.

NEED FOR HIGH LEVELS OF STIMULATION This strength drives some of the world's most creative and intuitive people. Richard Branson, founder of the Virgin Group, is known to be ADHD. And, like David Neeleman, Branson claims that his ADHD makes him what he is: a guy who will take big risks, who goes against the conventional thinking, and who loves intense physical challenges. It's hard to argue with a self-made billionaire!

DIVERGENT THINKING You tend to kick ideas around, offering suggestions, then modifying or embellishing upon them. Your wandering mind helps you notice things other people may miss and make new and interesting connections between ideas.

Living an Adventurous Life

You've heard for years that adventurous spirits need to conform—to learn to be more like everyone else. But there has to be a way that you can navigate life without giving up your dreams or your sense of self.

By understanding the positive traits that come with your personality—and being aware of the choices you can make every day to capitalize on those traits—you can set yourself on the path to a happier, more fulfilling life.

Careers

Office work typically requires sitting at a desk for many hours a day and focusing on a fixed set of tasks. While many adventurous spirits learn to survive and even excel in this kind of environment, it is hardly the best place for these people to really flourish.

My colleague Dietrich is a good example of this. When Dietrich was a freshly minted college graduate, he took a job as an accountant in a law firm. One of his tasks was to collect the billable hours from all of the accountants—not always a simple task in the days before email.

"I thought, hey, there are two hundred lawyers here and lots of them must be fun to talk to," Dietrich told me. "I'll spend five minutes talking to each one of them. So I would walk around the firm and do exactly that."

Although this sounds highly inefficient, Dietrich thinks it was probably the best and fastest method for him to gather the necessary data. Sitting at his desk and sorting through papers was frustrating and he was easily distracted. But by standing up and walking around, he managed to stay engaged, cut through some bureaucratic paperwork, and get the job done.

Unfortunately, Dietrich's boss didn't agree. "I'll never forget my boss telling me, 'You can't do that because you're distracting everybody,'" Dietrich told me.

"I said, 'Don't I finish the reports three days early each week? Don't I do them better than they've ever been done before?'"

"'Yes, you do,' my boss said, 'but I don't care. You just can't do it that way.'"

Lots of people who have an adventurous spirit just don't conform to the way things are "normally" done. Even if their method works just fine, or is even better than the standard way, others can have a hard time accepting it.

And of course there are some downsides. Adventurous people, for example, frequently have a difficult time paying close attention to details, can lose focus during a conversation, and don't always follow through on completing tasks. Dietrich admitted to some of these problems, especially difficulty paying attention. "In the middle of a conversation, I'll get caught on a thought and get lost in it," he said. "It's like I black out a little. That sounds really bad, I guess. But people I know well expect it of me. After a moment or two, I'll remember I'm having a conversation and I'll pop back in.

"I'll say, 'Hey, did you guys notice that I just zoned out?'

"And they'll say, 'Oh yeah.'"

It would be naïve to say that all you have to do is think about things differently to make this trait, or any other, into a positive. It's highly unlikely, for example, that colleagues, especially those who don't know you particularly well, will forgive you for zoning out every time they start talking. But awareness of these characteristics can help you keep them under control, and understanding the plus side can help you feel better about your profile. In Dietrich's story, it's clear to me that his difficulty with focus isn't simply a matter of boredom. He said he gets "caught" on a thought. Well, isn't that a characteristic of strong thinkers and successful entrepreneurs? Ideas pop into their heads at any time, often in response to things that other people say. You can almost see it happening, just as Dietrich's friends do.

Over time, Dietrich became acutely aware of how he operated and came to accept that his "abnormal" methods would never be fully accepted in an extremely traditional business setting. That's why he left his high-paying, career-track job in accounting to found a company. As I'll discuss later, it was actually Dietrich's combination of traits that made this the perfect career move—his self-focus gave him the leadership skills and charisma to found, lead, and sell a company (actually several companies), while magical thinking (see chapter 9) gave him the faith to believe in his business for years before he achieved financial success.

Dietrich's work as the leader of a small entrepreneurial business is perfect for his personality. He couldn't be happier with the path his life has taken. During a telephone interview, he said, "Right now, I'm looking at my computer, my cellphone is buzzing, and I've got the *Wall Street Journal* in front of me. But that doesn't mean I'm not interested in our conversation. That's just how I operate. I love it."

Dietrich is a great example of how to build a lifestyle around a dominant trait. When he gave up his job as an accountant to start his first company, he was certainly thinking outside the box. Although plenty of young people are interested in becoming entrepreneurs, their parents may not be so keen on the idea. They may tend to see entrepreneurial activity as too risky and unstable. And that's another thing that parents can do for their kids with an ascendant trait—think more deeply about jobs and careers and help their kids do the same. If they think that the only route forward in life runs through a cubicle, meds don't look so bad. But if they can catch a glimpse of people who have their trait and have followed very distinct and different paths, that's all to the good.

Soon enough, they'll be circumnavigating the globe, traveling to Jupiter, or founding a great new business!

Personal Life

Adventurous spirits tend to be sociable and fun-loving, often the life of the party—although you may not be able to get their attention for long! On the other hand, they can be hard to pin down, flighty, and sometimes unreliable when it comes to the details. Understanding how this trait affects your personal life and your relationships is profoundly important.

For example, people for whom being adventurous is superdominant have an increased tendency to get into car accidents.[8] Why is this? If we look at the traits associated with this group—easily distracted, talented multitaskers—it's easy to see why this would be the case. While it's fine to multitask at work, especially if it increases your ability to get things done, it can be a real problem on the road.

Awareness is essential. If you are doing something that requires focus for the long term, be aware of the potential risks. Turn off your cellphone so you won't be tempted to text while driving. (Texting while driving is as dangerous as drinking and driving!) If you are with a rowdy group of friends, consider letting someone else drive. And it's never a bad idea to take public transportation.

This may seem like a silly example, but the reasoning extends across the board. If you have a dominant trait like this one, social norms just may not apply. This holds for many aspects of life as an adventurous spirit. It's important to understand, for example, that your spontaneous, energetic, creative personality might be distracting to someone who is more OCD than ADHD. And when you're trying to collaborate with a colleague, it's essential that you realize that not everyone performs well when there is music playing and you are discussing several different topics at once. Here, compromise is key.

What about romantic relationships? I asked Seth (now in his

early twenties) about his love life. "I'm bad at long-term relation-ships," he admitted.

"Why do you say that?" I pressed.

"I get very, very bored," he said. "I just find relationships ex-tremely difficult because they get very routine very quickly."

When we spoke, Seth had just broken up with a girl whom he had dated for about a month. I asked him what happened. He said, "The first thing I tell a girl, once we start getting close, is, 'Hey, this is who I am. I enjoy my free time. I travel a lot. I just want to let you know right now that's how I am.' And I know a lot of people find that hard to accept."

Seth told me that this is exactly what happened during this lat-est relationship. At first, the woman had been understanding. "But after a few weeks, she started saying, 'No, you need to stay here this weekend.'"

Seth's frustration was palpable, and I could relate to how he felt. Trying to balance independence with a relationship can be tough.

When Seth decides he's ready for a long-term relationship, I would advise him to seek someone with the shy trait, someone who is content alone and won't mind, in fact may even enjoy, her alone time when he is off on an adventure. Someone who won't be freaked out when he announces, "Hey, I'm hitting the road for three or four months."

Many folks think that they would be better off with another ad-venturous spirit. Not the case! I do believe that opposites attract, so as a general rule two folks with the same dominant trait will find themselves struggling. If you are both constantly setting off on adventures around the world, then you will find little time for one another.

On the other hand, Seth told me that his next life plan is to ride a bicycle across China. An amazing goal! But not one that would work well if he was in a traditional relationship with a nine-to-five professional woman who sees normal as drinks after work on Tuesday and Thursday and dinner on Saturday.

At this stage in his life, Seth will have a difficult time getting involved with anyone who is too much in need of a traditional relationship. That's why the shy trait is such a great match. Many adventurous types welcome someone in their life who can be a source of stability when they return from their adventures. And shy people often appreciate a partner who can make himself scarce every once in a while! This is a great example of what I like to think of as complementary traits.

My general advice is to look for someone whose traits complement your own. But if you're already in a relationship, the most important thing is to understand how your dominant trait interacts with your partner's. Learn what makes you different, and what makes each of you great in your own way. ·

Conclusion: Are You Adventurous?

Are you adventurous? If so, you are one of a broad range of exciting and inspiring individuals. You carry the explorer gene—a genetic advantage that means you are primed for adventure and expedition. Whether you're leading the charge on a new creative enterprise at work, or you've given up a corporate career in order to visit every country in the world, there are many ways you can make your adventurous spirit work for you.

There are challenges that accompany being high on the ADHD continuum. Many social structures are built to confine big personalities like yours. People in positions of power don't always appreciate those who think (and act) outside the box called normal. And people who have opposite traits—those who are high in social anxiety, anxiety, or OCD—sometimes find your approach to life overwhelming or distracting. It's important to think about how you are handling these challenges and minimizing the troubling elements of your dominant personality trait. ·

Take some time to figure out how you're going to make your ascendant strengths work in your favor. Remember: You don't need to suppress your adventurous instincts. Let your energy, playfulness, and creativity shine. You'll be happier for it. And I think you'll find that if you embrace your personality, the people who care about you will learn to embrace it too.

perfectionist OCD

"OH MY GOD," people tell Alexis. "You're *ʌo* OCD."

Alexis is an event planner based in New York. When friends and colleagues refer to her as OCD, they're usually referring to the incredible attention to detail that she applies to her work in staging spectacular events for a major museum in the city. Or maybe they're talking about the carefully designed and perfectly plated meals that she serves at her catered events for other clients. Or they could be thinking of her precisely structured lifestyle, her perfectly balanced calendar of personal appointments and activities, her long-term planning of every element of her life.

Alexis has been a perfectionist since childhood. "One memory that sticks out to this day," she says, "is from when I went to boarding school in Connecticut and we all lived in dorm rooms. I remember, at fourteen or fifteen, taking great pride and care in making my bed. I arranged the pillows just the way I like them and tucked in the sheets with hospital corners. Then someone would come in and want to sit down on the bed because there wasn't a couch. I would say, 'God, no. *Do not ʌit on my bed.* It's perfect and I don't want an imprint on it.'"

Dorm-mates and friends didn't always understand Alexis' insistence on smooth blankets and neat hospital corners—but the habit continues to this day. "I'm not exempt from the rule," Alexis admitted to me. "Even if I need to sit on my bed to put on a pair of socks, I won't do it. I'll hop around, or lean against the wall. I just have this idea of perfectionism that I don't want tampered with."

When I asked Alexis whether her need for cleanliness, organization, and structure had ever caused her distress, she answered emphatically, "No, I can't say that it has."

That's clear evidence that Alexis does not suffer from obsessive-compulsive disorder. Diagnostically, OCD requires people to exhibit either obsessions or compulsions in a way that interferes with their life and causes them distress. This is not true for Alexis.

Instead, Alexis has built a successful life *around* her perfectionism. Living in New York City, a place so chaotic that many people get overwhelmed, she has imposed a structure that gives her comfort and stability. Eating, exercising, socializing, and working: It's all carefully planned, scheduled, and maintained. "I could not imagine waking up in the morning and not going to the gym." She's there six days a week.

Alexis is a seven on the OCD continuum—that's just how she is. For that reason, she says that working in event planning is "perfect for me. You're dealing with very high-level clients that have an eye for detail in certain things. If you don't meet their expectations, you're not doing your job." Alexis' personality isn't just an asset in her line of work—it's a necessity.

Perfectionism can serve a lot of people well. While it drives some nonperfectionists crazy ("Just let it go," they say), being a perfectionist means you are hyperneat, hyperorganized, immaculate, detail driven, and able to handle very complex tasks by breaking them down into their component parts. As a perfectionist, you exceed other people's expectations by setting high standards for yourself.

And that's a good thing.

The Continuum Model: Perfectionist

OBSESSIVE-COMPULSIVE CONTINUUM		
DISORGANIZED	DETAILED	OCD
0 3	5 7	10+
Absent	Dominant	Superdominant

Sometimes it seems as if obsessive-compulsive disorder, or OCD, is everywhere. As Alexis puts it, "It's gotten really mainstream now." Most of us are familiar with the stereotype of OCD, whether from familiarity with Melvin, Jack Nicholson's character in *As Good as It Gets,* or Adrian Monk, the obsessively clean detective in the TV show *Monk.* We all know the image of a socially awkward and overly anxious individual who washes his hands for hours, refuses to shake other people's hands, or performs a counting ritual. These are all common symptoms of OCD.

At the same time, as a mental disorder, OCD is often misunderstood and misrepresented by the popular media. Unlike ADHD, shyness, or anxiety, the stigma surrounding OCD is still strong. On TV and in films, people with OCD seem crazy, bizarre, weird, different—for most perfectionists, it's hard to look at Melvin or Monk and see a more extreme version of yourself.

Maybe that's why when we were conducting interviews for this book, my researchers and I had a difficult time finding people who fell in the category of perfectionism. Identifying these people was actually easy: We all know a perfectionist or two. But when I showed my interviewees the continuum model of perfectionism and they saw those three letters, OCD, at the far end of the spectrum, they got worried.

"You know," Kurt said insistently during his interview, "I don't know the official definition of these things. So it's hard for me to say." We'll hear more from Kurt in a minute.

Alexis agreed: "I'm not *really* OCD," she said.

But the truth is, even though popular culture still stigmatizes OCD, the psychiatric community has already begun to think of OCD as a spectrum disorder—one that has various levels of severity. The disorder is currently split into two: traditional obsessive-compulsive disorder (a phrase that dates from the time of Sigmund Freud), and the less severe obsessive-compulsive personality disorder. While OCD is associated with debilitating obsessions and compulsions, the personality disorder is characterized by a preoccupation with orderliness, perfectionism, and control.

What's more, the authors of the forthcoming DSM-V are currently planning to place obsessive-compulsive personality disorder on a personality continuum of its own, ranging from zero (no impairment) to four (severe impairment).

But the authors of the DSM-V are still wedded to a continuum model that moves from "normal" to four grades of "abnormal." I would never suggest that OCD *cannot* be a devastating disorder, because it can, and I've seen it. But the idea that increased perfectionism leads directly to an impaired life is absurd. For all the people who are perfectionists, a relatively small number are actually debilitated by their trait.

Most of us fall somewhere in the middle. And if, like Alexis, we find a perfect career or a perfect lifestyle, we can take advantage of our perfectionism to do great things. That's because the ascendant traits of perfectionism—perfectionists tend to be conscientious, organized, detailed, and focused—can be quite advantageous.

Imagine this: You're admitted to the emergency room of a hospital in a city that's not your own. Your medical records are halfway across the country, and you are in no condition to recall all the relevant information the nurses want from you. Thank goodness the person who designed the IT system for the hospital was detail oriented and careful to the point of obsession. That attention to detail may be the thing that saves your life.

Or imagine this: You're on a plane somewhere over the Atlantic Ocean. We tend to forget what a miracle flight is—but airplanes are complex machines and our lives are dependent on their proper functioning. Big-picture thinkers didn't design the intricate gauges and machinery that keep you in flight. It took a perfectionist mind.

Perfectionists make great engineers, managers, planners, and organizers of all kinds. But lots of glamorous careers depend on perfectionist personalities too. Fashion designers such as Vera Wang are known for their focus on little things. As Wang said in an interview,

> I'm obsessed with details and how they relate to the wearer. I visualize women. I do this with all my products. A woman can be an athlete; she can be a classic, traditional individual; she can be vampish. Any or all these personality traits can be part of the same woman.[1]

Sounds like Vera Wang knows a thing or two about continuum traits—and perfectionism.

My favorite perfectionist career is that of detective. Adrian Monk, of the hit TV show *Monk,* is an extreme example: He is known for his obsession with hand sanitizer and symmetry, as well as for his talent for solving crimes. All the great detectives (fictional and otherwise) have an incredible eye for detail. Who said being a perfectionist can't be a glamorous life?

Redefining OCD

Genuine OCD is one of the more devastating and misunderstood disorders among the continuum traits and it supposedly affects, in varying degrees, 2 to 3 percent of the population.[2] (Again, I think this percentage is inflated due to overdiagnosis.) For this reason, before I get into the details of the OCD continuum and its corresponding ascendant strengths, I want to explain some of the nuances and complexity of the disorder.

OCD is called obsessive-compulsive disorder for a reason: People with OCD suffer from both *obsessions* and *compulsions.* In the DSM and medical lexicon, these terms have very specific meanings. *Obsessions* are defined by the DSM as recurrent or persistent thoughts that are experienced as intrusive—that is, they appear in your mind unbidden, and once they've appeared, they don't simply fade away. If you leave the house, get on the bus, and think: *Oh no, what if I forgot to turn off the stove?* that's perfectly healthy. We all worry about things like that from time to time.

If you can't stop thinking about that stove—if, no matter how much you try, it stays in your mind so that you're totally consumed all day long about that darn stove—then it's an obsession. To qualify as an obsession, the thought has to cause you distress and you have to be aware that it's unreasonable. Maybe you didn't even turn on the stove this morning. Maybe you double-checked three times on your way out the door. Maybe you start thinking about that stove every morning. You feel anxious and distraught about the situation. You jump off the bus after one stop and run back home just to make sure. It takes you longer and longer—several hours, even—to reassure yourself that everything's okay and you can go to work. Now you have an obsession.

How do you cope with your obsession? *Compulsions* are one way that people with OCD deal with an obsession like a fear of germs, a fear of illness, or a need for symmetry. Compulsions can be loosely associated with an obsession: You're obsessed with germs, so you wash your hands compulsively twenty times a day. But they can also have little or no relation to reality, as when Melvin of *As Good as It Gets* flicks the lights on and off three times in order to ward off disease.

What exactly do folks with OCD fear? OCD obsessions vary from person to person, but they tend to fall into several general categories:

Fear of germs (50 percent)

Fear of life-threatening illness (33 percent)

Need for order and symmetry (32 percent)

Recurrent thoughts about committing aggressive acts (31 percent)

Recurrent thoughts about inappropriate sexual acts (24 percent)[3]

Above all, I hope that this list demonstrates the complexity and the challenge of life with obsessive-compulsive disorder. Because the people who suffer from this disorder recognize the irrational nature of their obsessions and their compulsions, they can suffer from fear and self-doubt on top of their illness. Two out of every three OCD patients have experienced at least one major depressive episode in their lives.[4]

My major point here: OCD is a complex and often devastating illness that varies from person to person, and throughout a person's lifetime. It can appear in childhood and fade out during adulthood, or it can get more severe over time. Anxiety or stress can exacerbate the condition. And certain treatments can help make symptoms more manageable.

Today, most people with OCD are given a combination of therapeutic and medical treatments. SSRIs (selective serotonin reuptake inhibitors) can help reduce symptoms of OCD. So can behavioral and cognitive therapies. Behavioral therapy is often done in situ: The patient is exposed to the source of his obsession, and then encouraged not to respond with a compulsive behavior. Cognitive therapy is more about changing the way you think (cognition equals thought), learning to reframe an obsession so it becomes less debilitating. Learning to understand your OCD trait and live a perfectionist lifestyle, I hope, can also help you turn obsessive and compulsive behavior into a positive.

It's been done before. A good example is the TV celebrity Howie Mandel. He has spoken publicly about his struggles with OCD and his obsession with germs. He has all kinds of "quirky" behaviors that he uses to help him cope. Not only does his shaved head make him feel cleaner, his habit of fist bumping, rather than handshaking, is another of his germ-avoidance strategies. Even with these quirks, Mandel has managed to be a significant force in show business for more than thirty years. In addition to his hit television shows, he has performed in some two hundred concerts a year, and has written the bestselling memoir *Here's the Deal: Don't Touch Me.* It tells the story of Howie's struggle with OCD and ADHD and the role his traits have played in his professional and personal life.[5]

For people at the extreme end of the perfectionist spectrum, like Howie, life can be a struggle—but that's no reason you can't be fulfilled and successful too.

An Evolutionary Imperative

Like many psychological disorders, OCD has a genetic component. Studies have shown that 3 to 12 percent of first-degree relatives of those with OCD share the trait; studies of identical twins with OCD similarly suggest a genetic factor.[6] This begs the question: If obsessive-compulsive disorder is really such a bad thing, then why does it exist? Why didn't evolutionary forces weed out the OCD among us centuries ago?

This question is flawed: Evolution, we all know, doesn't work that way. Lots of horrible things—cancer, heart disease, etc.—are passed down through our genes. It would be a mistake to think evolution only picks the good genes.

But heart disease and cancer tend to appear relatively late in people's lives. In prehistoric times, women and men began to have children around the age of thirteen, so they only had to survive until puberty in order to pass on their genes. Genetic mutations that would eventually lead to cancer didn't matter at all in the evolutionary scheme.

But OCD can appear in childhood or early adolescence. It doesn't wait until you're past childbearing age to show its face. In fact, research shows that OCD is associated with decreased fecundity—a lower chance of having children and passing on your genetic material.

So why has OCD survived the pressures of natural selection? A group of scientists at the University of Manitoba call this the OCD paradox. One possibility, they say, is that OCD is like sickle cell anemia. It could be closely tied to a gene that is so good for us, it has survived despite its negative consequences. Sickle cell anemia, for example, comes along with a resistance to malaria. The positive trait (surviving malaria) outweighed the negative (sickle cell anemia, in a small portion of the population) and the gene survived. The problem, and it's a big one, with this theory is that OCD doesn't come with resistance to malaria—or any other benefit that we currently know about.[7]

Instead, the scientists from Manitoba suggest, maybe OCD is positive *in itself.* Some social animals, like bees or ants, exhibit a kind of specialization in which some have bodies suited for harvesting, some for reproducing, and some for war. Natural selection has favored the development of diversity in this instance.

If OCD is seen as an "ancient behavioral specialization," as these scientists propose, then it's possible to understand how certain OCD symptoms actually could have benefited a Stone Age village, without burdening the entire society with OCD.

What are the evolutionary benefits of OCD symptoms? One is compulsive washing. In a time or place where people didn't even know about bacteria, there was no *rational* reason for anyone to keep things hygienic or sanitary. But if even one member of a tribe insisted on it, the whole community would have been cleaner and healthier—without knowing why. And in fact, there are still tribal communities that have washing and cleaning rituals even though they don't understand the concept of germs and bacterial infections. Could those rituals have originated in someone with OCD?

Obsessive checking could also have many uses. Imagine this: You live in a tribal community in a tropical rain forest along the equator. Your health and diet depend on your ability to cook your food. But you don't know how to make fire. All you know is how to keep the fire you have alive. If it goes out you might have to trek miles into the wilderness in search of a passing tribe that can share its fire with you. An obsessive checker would never let the fire die out. That could keep the whole Stone Age village alive.

Or consider hoarding. Most of the time, we think of hoarders as people who live in cluttered and unmanageable apartments, unable to move, to cook, or to clean. But what if the thing these people were hoarding was essential to a tribe? What if a hoarder kept huge stashes of food during a time of famine? For survival, the whole Stone Age village might have depended on that individual hoarder.[8]

Actually, this isn't just speculation. I've successfully treated hoarders by helping them transform their compulsion into a useful practice. One woman I worked with more than twenty years ago managed to begin a collection of bottle tops, corks, and cans, which today is worth a staggering amount of money. Recently she found me on Facebook and thanked me profusely. She created what amounts to a retirement fund by taking advantage of what most people consider the symptom of a debilitating disorder. Even people at the far end of the continuum can find good and productive uses for their trait.

Ascendant Strengths

Some degree of perfectionism is healthy and can be advantageous in both your work and social lives. Perfectionism confers the following ascendant strengths:

DRIVE You know how to set realistic, attainable goals—and how to reach them.

THOROUGHNESS You apply great attention to detail, with the ability to hyperfocus, and you demonstrate a careful approach to doing things.

NEATNESS AND ORGANIZATION Are your pens grouped by length, color, and type? Envelopes and papers stacked by shape, size, and color? Great! This level of organization can help you be more productive; you don't have to search endlessly for things because you know exactly where they are.

HIGH STANDARDS You wouldn't get obsessive about a project unless you wanted to do well. Obsessive-compulsiveness can be a reminder that you wish to succeed.

FOCUS As long as your obsessions don't tip over into the extreme, they can help you concentrate on the task at hand. People high in this trait tend to be focused on work, always arrive on time, and can be counted on to do the job in a prompt and reliable way.

Living a "Perfect" Life

Living a "perfect life." That really speaks to the challenges, and the benefits, of a dominant perfectionist personality. If you're a seven or above on the OCD continuum, you are probably familiar with the problem of perfectionism. On the one hand, being detail oriented, focused, and committed to the task at hand is a good thing. It's necessary for high-quality performance, no matter what you're working for. Musicians and engineers alike know the necessity of patience, persistence, and hard work in pursuit of excellence.

But of course, "perfection" is an elusive goal. Nobody's perfect—and at some point we all have to be able to say "good enough" and move on. Otherwise we will never finish anything at all! The pursuit of perfection in itself just leads to frustration and disappointment.

You can find a good balance, however. It is possible to pursue excellence in your daily life without losing sight of the bigger picture. In your career and in your relationships, you can learn to identify and minimize the challenges that come with your personality, while taking advantage of your ascendant strengths. It might not be "perfect"—but that sounds pretty ideal to me.

Careers

I spoke about the importance of care, precision, and attention to detail to success in many careers. Alexis described her job as the perfect one for her, and in fact, her personality is perfect for her job.

Kurt wasn't quite as lucky as Alexis. A passionate wordsmith and lover of the minute elements of language that make up the written word, Kurt thought he had found his calling when he began to pursue a Ph.D. in English literature.

But literary study, it turns out, is not the same as an academic career. "Two things got in my way," Kurt told me. "One was that I wasn't a very good writer." He laughed. "Writing was always a problem for me because I would have a very clear notion of what I wanted to say and it was very specific. But I could never just write down ideas and then hone them afterward." Instead, he would get stuck for hours trying to figure out the perfect sentence. He was totally paralyzed.

Kurt faced the same problem as a teacher. When he was grading papers, he started imagining what the ideal paper could be. Before he knew it, he said, "I would feel compelled to try to rewrite the whole paper." It got to the point where he felt that his desk literally repelled him, like the wrong end of a magnet. Kurt's love for language, and his passion for the minute details of research, were one thing, but the daily work of being a professional academic was a whole other story.

One day, some friends stopped by with a newspaper advertisement for a job working as a clock repairman. Even in the 1960s, clock repair wasn't exactly a common profession. "It was probably the first and last time there had been an advertisement for a clockmaker in the last thirty years." Kurt hadn't even been looking for a job. But it was obvious to him that something had to change. He submitted his application.

The choice of clock making wasn't as random as it might sound. Kurt had always loved working with his hands—he had done piano repair and was learning to build musical instruments. He loved the problem-solving element of the work, and the attention to detail that it required. He had even fixed a clock for a friend once, just for fun. When he was offered the job, Kurt left academia for good.

Kurt's story is an inspiring one. What started out as an odd job at four dollars per hour eventually became a full-fledged career in machining. Kurt now runs a successful small business where he says his passion for precision is perfectly at home. In machining as in writing, he explained, you can have an incredibly specific vision of what you want to achieve.

At the same time, as a machinist, there are well-defined parameters that help Kurt keep his obsessive perfectionism under control. While an essay can be edited forever, clients who order machined parts specify the degree of perfection—say, one hundredth of a millimeter. Once Kurt has achieved that level of perfection, he can stop. The work matches his interests and his personality without overwhelming him and pushing him further down the continuum.

I was happy to learn from Kurt about the way that he found success by embracing his trait, but there's a lesson to be learned from this story that extends beyond the details of Kurt's career path. Like Kurt, when I was a younger man, I found myself drawn to a field that wasn't right for me. I got caught up in a romantic and passionate dream: I decided I was going to travel the world, hunting for diamonds.

"Sure, Dale," you're thinking, "you're the classic adventurous personality." You're right! The vision of traveling the world— seeking glamour and glory and beauty—attracted me. I flew to California to study at the Gemological Institute of America and learned how to judge diamonds. I loved the acquisition of new knowledge, I was excited by my vision for the future, and I had a great time at the institute. Before I knew it, I was on a plane to Tel Aviv, ready to buy diamonds.

As it turns out, however, the day-to-day life of diamond hunting is not as glamorous as the TV version. On that first trip, I arrived in Tel Aviv after midnight and by six o'clock the next morning I was in a series of offices in the diamond district, examining stones. For the next ten hours, I sat in place and evaluated diamonds. And so it went for the entire week. My personality trait, as you know, is not the type to sit still for long. I was restless, frustrated, and, frankly, bored.

At the time I didn't understand what had gone wrong. Like Kurt, I didn't really know much about personality traits, and it didn't occur to me that my profile wasn't a good match for this field. All I knew was that I had to get out. And I soon did.

I've been fairly successful in my many ventures—as a psychiatrist, a poker player, and now as an advocate for a new way of thinking about personality traits. Over the years, I think I can say that I've moved closer and closer to a lifestyle that meshes perfectly with my own unique personality profile. I haven't gone chasing diamonds recently, though sometimes I still miss the idea of what I thought that would represent.

This is Kurt's story too. Out of his failure as an academic, Kurt found professional success. Over the years, he slowly began to recognize his true strengths and how to use them. When he found a job that suited him, he stayed in it—and what at first appeared to be a major risk turned into a successful lifestyle choice.

I hope that's a lesson we all can learn from.

Personal Life

Say Kurt wants to buy a camera.

When most of us set out to buy a camera, we usually do a little bit of research, maybe shop around for a while, make a decision, and then make the purchase.

Not Kurt. Here's how he goes at it. "I start researching," he said. "And given the American way, the number of options at my command is almost infinite. So that means I can spend a long time researching the best camera for me. I spend hours considering all the various options and thinking about why this camera might be better for me than that camera. I'm not a professional photographer. I really just want to take snapshots. But there are so many other kinds of pictures I could take with different kinds of cameras. With this one, I could get great shots of wildlife. Well, maybe I would want to take shots of wildlife. That's possible. I like wildlife.

Oh, and look, this camera enables me to take movies too. I might want to shoot movies someday. So I get more and more into this, and then I get more and more options, the options proliferate and it becomes very hard to make a decision. So then I say, well, I've spent three months researching cameras, maybe I don't really need a camera at all. My original enthusiasm for cameras starts to dissipate. And soon I realize that I could live without a camera."

The next thing Kurt knows, he's looking at a beautiful view after a long hike, or attending an event with his family, and thinking, *I wish I had a camera.*

Perfectionism can be frustrating for you and for your loved ones. If you find yourself faced with the challenge of living a perfectionist life—if you feel as if an obsession is truly standing in your way, whether it's keeping you from purchasing a camera, or whether it's more profound—I recommend that you follow the three R's: recognize, reorganize, redirect.

Before I describe the three R's in a bit more detail, let me say that these three steps can help you with any situation or problem—not just perfectionism or any of the other eight traits. Whatever issue you're struggling with—such as low self-esteem, anger, or fear of confrontation—a good way to think about it and an effective way to develop an action plan for dealing with it is by carefully going through the three R's. (I developed these in my practice years ago, but others use them as well and have written about them—including Ian Spencer, who expanded on them to include two more R's: redo and repeat—so these concepts may be familiar to you. If so, good!) Here they are:

RECOGNIZE First, you have to pay close attention to the problem itself and define it for yourself. With perfectionism, for example, you probably realize that you have a tendency toward obsession. But even if you are aware that you can sometimes be obsessive, it's easy to get caught up in an obsession before you know it. So the first step to managing obsession is to always be aware of your thoughts and emotions and to identify ones that seem characteristic of obsessive-compulsive behavior.

Try to remove that kind of thinking from your mental and emotional makeup. To do so, consider writing them down in a diary or notebook, so you can look back and reflect over time. In the case of Kurt's camera story, for example, he might write *I must find the perfect camera.*

REORGANIZE Now that you have identified the troublesome thoughts and have written them down, you can more easily figure out how to reorganize them. The goal is to find the positive in what you have always thought of as negative. Kurt, for example, might say to himself: *It sure will be great to get some photos of my niece and her new husband at their wedding.* Or, *The last time I made a big purchase, which was a TV, it worked out great. I'm so glad I have it! The same will probably be true of the camera.*

REDIRECT The final step is to find a new and more positive direction for your concerns. One way to do so is to distract yourself. Deliberately turn your attention elsewhere. Take a walk. Clean out the attic. Eat a favorite food. Call a friend. Plan a trip. Go to the gym. Do something, almost anything, that reliably gives you some pleasure and will not lead you to more of the same distress.

Kurt's an avid cyclist, so he often steps away from the computer and goes for a bike ride if he's feeling overwhelmed. Then he makes himself a cup of his favorite Darjeeling tea and returns to the task, refreshed and ready to decide which camera to purchase.

Kurt's wife also supports him to make decisions and push through his sometimes obsessive or compulsive days. "One of the qualities that my wife has is that she's not so obsessed about things," Kurt said. "That makes it kind of relaxing, because while I can get obsessed about things, she doesn't."

There is one other benefit that Kurt mentioned in regard to being married to someone less obsessive than he is. "She can just do things without having to be obsessed about them. So before we go on vacation, *she* can buy a camera, any camera!"

The three R's worked well for Kurt. I have seen them work for many, many people (including me) who have used the process to deal with a wide range of personal problems.

Conclusion: Are You Perfectionist?

If you fall somewhere on the high end of the OCD continuum—if perfectionism is your dominant trait—then you're probably familiar with some of the challenges of living with this trait. But have you thought carefully about how your ascendant strengths can be an asset in your working life? Or what role they might play in your relationships?

If perfectionism is your dominant personality trait, then you carry genes that have been historically essential to the survival of the human species. Your ascendant strengths—thoroughness, neatness, high standards, and focus—have been advantageous to humanity for hundreds of thousands of years. And they continue to play a vital role in today's society.

If perfectionism is your dominant personality trait, take some time to think about where this trait comes from and what role it plays in your life. Ask yourself whether you are using your detail-oriented personality, or whether you think of it as a disability or a problem. And then figure out whether there is anything you can do to better embrace your trait. Pick up that detail-oriented hobby you've always wanted to do. Sign up to be the treasurer or event planner for a charity in your community. If this is your dominant trait, then your focus and attention to detail put you at a huge advantage. Make sure you're not trying to suppress your trait. It's your greatest asset—don't you think it's time to embrace it?

FOUR shy SOCIAL ANXIETY DISORDER

SHYNESS IS NOT one of my dominant traits.

I am gregarious and charismatic. I love performing. I love meeting new people—and in fact that's a big part of my job as a psychiatrist and as a news commentator.

My childhood friend Lorraine is the opposite. While my calendar is filled to the brim with professional meetings and social engagements, Lorraine works at home and enjoys just a couple of outside activities a week. While I thrive in group settings, Lorraine does her best work when she's on her own.

Lorraine, who is fifty-two years old and lives in the Deep South, was a nerdy kid who always had a few close friends, but not any large groups of friends. She was a huge reader—and remains so today, with a Kindle that is overflowing with books and other reading material—and was also very creative. She was an art major in college.

When Lorraine realized she could not support herself with the money she was making in the arts, she went back to school to get her law degree. After graduation, she got snapped up by a big law firm. Then came trouble.

"I don't like working in offices and I don't like having a boss," Lorraine said with her characteristic straightforwardness. Lots of people find it hard to adjust to a work environment where their time is tightly controlled. But for Lorraine, working in an office ran against her very nature: Lorraine's an eight on the social anxiety continuum. "I am always so nervous in an office environment," she says.

It didn't help that she had a "nightmare of a boss" who didn't allow her any freedoms. "He got furious that I was working out on my lunch hour. That's how controlling the guy was." She eventually got fired. But Lorraine thinks that was for the best because it opened the door for her to start her own niche legal business. She researches and writes briefs for attorneys to use in appeals cases. "I do a lot of plaintiff personal injury work trying to help people get recoveries for their injuries. And I find it very rewarding. I'm very lucky, I think."

It takes a lot of courage to be an independent professional—maybe even more so for a single woman than for a man—and I respect Lorraine for that. Hers was a smart move. Her shy personality was obviously not suited for a career that depended on her ability to relate to others in a large group setting. But now she is so in demand that she doesn't even need to market herself to get work. (A good thing, because she doesn't like the crowds at places like the local bar association meetings.) Sure, if she did some extra marketing she could probably make more money. But she's held on to some clients for fifteen or twenty years just by being so skilled at what she does behind the scenes. She helps make those attorneys—who, unlike her, *do* love the spotlight—look really great in front of the appellate judges.

As I'll discuss more in this chapter, Lorraine's success in her work and in other areas of her life is directly related to her shyness. She showed incredible strength from within when she took a bad situation—a difficult boss and the resulting unemployment—and turned it into an opportunity to capitalize on who she really is. And in fact she has done that many times as she has faced difficulties in her life.

If shyness is dominant in your life, I hope this chapter will help you see that a quiet life is not a bad one—and help you tap in to the powerful resource of your strength from within.

The Continuum Model: Shyness

SOCIAL ANXIETY CONTINUUM				
EXTROVERTED		INDEPENDENT		SOCIAL ANXIETY
0	3	5	7	10+
Absent		Dominant		Superdominant

Let's look at someone further along on the social anxiety continuum to see the range that is possible.

The following is an email I received on my website from a thirty-nine-year-old woman, whom I'll call Debra:

As long as I can remember, I've had difficulties in social situations. In school, I would keep to myself. The thought of having to speak in front of the class or sit in the lunchroom with all the others would send me into a panic. I had a few close friends, but without them by my side, I felt like everyone was staring at me.

I find myself avoiding even the people I love, with the exception of my husband and children. I stress over situations where I have to be around others: birthday parties, school functions, and so forth.

I try really hard to overcome these fears. Recently, I volunteered at my daughter's school because I want so badly to be a good mother, but my stomach was tied in knots the whole time.

If I see an old friend out somewhere, I avoid them if possible. At the grocery store, I will go hide down another aisle, for example. When my phone rings, I usually only answer if it's my mom or husband. The weird thing is that sometimes, but not very often, I feel normal and will answer the phone and talk for quite a while with friends.

I have these days where I feel good and want to be with others, but they are few and far between. I also have become very irritable with my family, snapping at my husband and kids over the simplest things. When in large crowds such as at the mall, I feel like I'm just going to explode. I always get irritable and nervous in these situations. I don't mean to be this way, but I just get so nervous and in a panic. I said when my daughter started school that I would get a job. She's now in kindergarten and the fear of actually going to ask for a job, have an interview and have to be around new people, is more than I can bear. I know I have a problem and need to get help.

As anyone can see, Debra is shy. In fact, it seems to me that at this point in her life Debra is a nine or ten on the social anxiety continuum. Her shyness has become superdominant—it is now so extreme that it keeps her from living her life to the fullest, and it's making her severely unhappy.

From her email, of course, I can't tell exactly how superdominant her trait is, and to what extent she needs psychiatric treatment or medication. (I would never make a diagnosis on the basis of an email alone.) But Debra's condition sounds as if it is close to the psychiatric ailment known as social anxiety disorder.

Social anxiety disorder, which is also sometimes called social phobia, is essentially defined as being afraid of other people or social situations.[1] You've probably seen this disorder portrayed in advertisements for drugs aimed at reducing social anxiety. In those ads, unhappy-looking men and women stand in the corner during a party, while a voice-over explains social anxiety, asking if *you* have ever felt unhappy in a social situation or if you have ever felt you are missing out on the fun of life.

I'd say that meds are the last place you should turn if you find social situations stressful or if you feel that you are "missing out on the fun of life." First you need to take a real, sustained look at your personality and at the small changes you can make to bring your life more in line with your dominant traits. At the end of this chapter I'll recommend some actions to take.

But there are medications that can relieve the worst symptoms of social anxiety and help you move toward the middle of the continuum. People with social anxiety experience debilitating *fear* of any situation that might put them under public scrutiny (like a performance, a party, even a date). And they experience severe anxiety or panic when they actually attend these events. When it gets really severe, social anxiety can make it hard for these people to maintain a relationship, hold a job, or complete basic daily tasks.

Debra is an example of a person who experiences social anxiety in a debilitating way. I would advise her (and on my website, I did) to go see a psychiatrist who can learn more about her, consider her symptoms more closely, and determine what she should do to alleviate her suffering. If she does have severe social anxiety, anti-anxiety medications might be a helpful tool, along with changes in lifestyle and cognitive-behavioral therapy. These tools would help her become a more healthy six or seven on the social anxiety continuum. But Debra will never be a zero or a one. Debra, and anyone else with social anxiety, has to go through the sometimes difficult challenge of learning to embrace her dominant personality trait.

With a little bit of help from doctors, people with full-blown social anxiety disorder can become role models for what a shy lifestyle can be.

Redefining Social Anxiety Disorder

As a society, we benefit from people who operate on the sidelines. People whom some think of as "wallflowers" may in fact be our great observers and interpreters. Many authors, such as Agatha Christie and Harper Lee, are known to have been extremely shy. But through their words, they told stories that changed the world. Harper Lee's *To Kill a Mockingbird,* for example, is a profound commentary on American society. It won the Pulitzer Prize, was voted one of the greatest American books of all time, and is taught in classrooms around the country. But Harper Lee is known for almost never appearing in public.

It's not just writers. The actress Kim Basinger is said to have taken ballet lessons as a kid to help her learn to cope with her paralyzing shyness. Miami Dolphins running back Ricky Williams, two-time All-American athlete and winner of the Heisman trophy, was diagnosed with social anxiety disorder. Although Williams was a superstar on the field, he was known for giving interviews with his helmet on and his visor down. "Ricky's just a different guy," his teammate Joe Horn explained.

And of course, perhaps the most celebrated shy people in today's society are the computer nerds. As teenagers, they were teased for being nerdy and socially awkward, spending their weekends writing code while their more gregarious counterparts played sports and went to parties. But the time and energy that these kids put into their studies make them experts who are way ahead of the curve. We need only look as far as Bill Gates or Mark Zuckerberg to see the way that shy individuals can turn their unique personalities into an opportunity for success. It's been said that Zuckerberg, despite his fame and considerable fortune, doesn't like to be on TV because he "panics" in front of a camera. And of course, social networking sites such as Zuckerberg's Facebook can be useful tools to help shy people maneuver through life's challenges. Not bad for a shy guy.

You can run away, but you can't run away from yourself. You can try to flee a lot of things, but you always bring yourself along—and so you will be happiest in life when you accept who you are and work with your true strengths.

That's why the number-one tenet of this book is the ancient Greek aphorism *Know thyself.* Once you know who you are—once you know your dominant trait(s)—you have a choice. You can fight with yourself every day to try to be like everybody else. Or you can choose to embrace your dominant personality trait.

An Evolutionary Imperative

What is shyness? In 2003, Israeli scientists thought they had identified the root cause of shyness when they discovered the so-called shyness gene. To identify shy children, the scientists interviewed a hundred schoolchildren, their families, and their teachers. Then they analyzed their DNA. They found that shy children tended to have a particular gene—the long allele of the 5-HTTLPR polymorphism. This is one of the genes that is also associated with anxiety, and there's no surprise there—anxiety and shyness are surely closely linked.[2] (That's why some people have labeled shyness "social anxiety," and in the DSM-IV, it falls under the general category of an anxiety disorder.)

It makes intuitive sense that shyness would be associated with certain genes—and in fact, heritability studies show that shyness is a genetically inherited personality trait. The contribution of genetics to social anxiety is thought to be as high as 51 percent.[3] And new research suggests that the genes associated with anxiety affect specific activation patterns—specific ways of thinking and responding to stress—that occur in the "emotion center" of our brain, a part of the brain known as the amygdala.[4]

So genes can affect the way we feel in social situations. But studies of identical twins show that shyness is much more complex than the genetics involved. When scientists studied pairs of identical and fraternal twins, they found that although identical twins have the same exact genetic makeup, they aren't equally shy. As usual, environmental factors play a role as well.

Still, any trait that has a genetic source suggests evolution, and it's interesting to think about what might make people shy. Is it possible that there's an evolutionary benefit to shyness?

No doubt you can guess what my position will be on this subject. I'm sure that there's an evolutionary benefit to shyness—and evolutionary scientists back me up. Anxiety is widely thought to be caused by an increased awareness of risk or danger. It's easy to imagine why that would be useful, especially in more life-threatening times. When a saber-toothed tiger might have been just around the bend, and when even a minor wound could be deadly, heightened sensitivity to risk was a lifesaver.

Social anxiety is thought to come from awareness of a more subtle danger. Instead of carnivorous beasts or warfare or storms, social anxiety generally comes from a heightened increase in awareness of social dangers. People who are socially anxious tend to be better able to identify changes in facial cues than the rest of us—especially when those cues make them feel threatened. They are more likely to recognize how people are feeling, making them unusually empathic. And they are hyperaware of how one person's behavior can cause social conflict.[5]

Why is this important? Stone Age villages were extremely hierarchical and social norms were much stricter than they are today. You might say that the box called normal was even more restrictive than it is now. The smallest social mistake could lead to ostracism or exile—and exile would probably lead to death. Being aware of social cues, and being able to avoid social conflict, was literally a life-or-death imperative.

Shyness is also a heritable personality trait in the animal kingdom. Take the dumpling squid, for example. These sea creatures can show genetic disposition to be bold or shy as they develop. When in a stressful or high-risk situation, their personality traits seem to become even stronger. Shy squid stay shy, and bold squid get bolder. One proposal the scientists make: Shy squid and bold squid complement each other in the wild because they are suited for different kinds of environments. Bold squid bravely venture into feeding grounds where no squid has gone before, while shy squid stay in their safe haven—and resources are shared by all.[6]

In both squid and humans, shyness has apparently evolved as a kind of safety mechanism. What's more, shy people tend to have a number of important traits that make them an essential part of society. Some scientists have suggested that shyness is a servile characteristic, but I think they are too heavily influenced by the current idea that shyness is a weakness or even a disorder. Shy people aren't society's servants. They are our writers, computer programmers, artists, philosophers, inventors, and spiritual leaders. They may not seek fame and glory, but they are of vital importance as observers and interpreters of the social experience.

What's more, shy people tend to have what I call a "strength from within." It's a common fallacy that shyness comes from an underlying insecurity in yourself. In fact, shy people can be incredibly self-confident and exert a great independent force on the course of their lives. That's a strength that can lead you to do great things. It's only in today's narcissistic culture that marketing has us all convinced that outgoing and talkative equal "good" and shyness equals "bad."

Ascendant Strengths

Some degree of introversion is healthy and can be advantageous in both your work and social lives. Shyness confers the following ascendant strengths:

KEEN LISTENING SKILLS You probably prefer listening and absorbing information to being talkative, a quality that serves you well in relationships and at work. Because you may spend more time listening than you do talking, you tend to notice details and remember important facts about the people you meet, then use this information in a thoughtful and deliberate way. This is a sign of an effective communicator.

SENSITIVITY You are usually attentive to nuances, to subtle differences in people and situations, and have empathy toward others—great strengths for building solid relationships. You tend to be considerate and sensitive—just the kind of person someone else who's shy wants to meet! You also can develop deep friendships and have strong people skills in small-group or one-on-one situations.

DELIBERATE, THOUGHTFUL DECISION MAKING You often process ideas internally and need to reflect before taking action.

INDEPENDENCE You usually work well with little supervision. You are focused, content working alone, and generally don't mind working behind the scenes or allowing others to take the spotlight. You can make a good employee if put in the right spot, assigned to the proper duties, and given a chance to prove yourself.

PRODUCTIVE SOLITUDE You tend to enjoy your alone time, using it for self-reflection, and appreciate quiet space when you are trying to concentrate. A while back, I did an informal survey of my patients just to see how many of them had ever been out to dinner by themselves. I learned that fewer than 5 percent (one in twenty!) of them had. Most people do not like to be alone, largely because we are a couple-centric society. TV ads, books, and movies all tell us that we're losers if we're not in a romantic relationship—another unfortunate stigma. The ability to enjoy one's own company is a tremendous asset.

CARING. You generally show a caring and considerate attitude when working with others, in relationships, and in family situations.

Living a Quiet Life

Being shy isn't always easy. Our society is built around social institutions, and especially in today's self-promoting, narcissistic culture, there is a lot of pressure on all of us to conform to a certain personality: one that is gregarious, charming, and fun to be around. The college student who prefers to stay in on a Saturday night, or the woman who lives alone and turns down neighborly invitations, is considered boring, aloof, or seen as a loser.

Caroline Knapp, author of the well-known memoir *Drinking: A Love Story,* wrote several articles about shyness. She reported that her neighbors began talking behind her back after she turned down yet another backyard cookout. "They think I'm a snob? Superior? Can't they tell I'm just shy?" she asked.[7]

After the years of self-discovery chronicled in her memoir, Knapp was in a place in her life where she could handle that kind of criticism and try to take action. But the vast majority of shy people take a different tack: They try to suck it up and get over it. They attend those backyard events, despite the almost crippling suffering it causes them. They go out to college parties on Saturday nights and they see psychiatrists to have their shyness treated.

Shyness and Addiction

In some cases, shy people seek out tools to help relieve their social phobia—tools such as alcohol, marijuana, or tobacco. A "social lubricant" is what some people call alcohol, but we all know there is a delicate line between having a drink to ease your discomfort and developing a full-scale addiction. Knapp is far from alone in this behavior. Lorraine also spoke with me about her own struggles with addiction.

"When I was younger," she said in our interview, "I had a pretty bad alcohol problem."

Lorraine confirmed what I said earlier, that alcohol can become a tool for anxious people. "A lot of people drink to take the edge off their social anxiety or loneliness," she explained. "So if you're a very introverted person, that's one way you can cope with being lonely." For many years, this was Lorraine's situation. She was in a bad marriage with an alcoholic and she struggled to get by.

The most inspiring thing about Lorraine's story? Her internal strength made it possible for her to beat the addiction that for many years had dominated her life.

Lorraine had been trying to cut down on her drinking for some time. "I tried to moderate the drinking, but I found that didn't work." What really struck me was her difficulty with Alcoholics Anonymous. I often forget the degree to which our society is structured for people who do well in groups. AA is a group-oriented program, and didn't work for Lorraine.

"I didn't go to Alcoholics Anonymous because I'm not a joiner," she said. "I went to one AA meeting and it was so depressing I couldn't handle it."

A group program like AA wasn't going to help Lorraine because being with all those people compounded the problem. Although she is a spiritual person, Lorraine felt the same way about going to church. She preferred to pursue her faith in her own private way. That was also the source of her strength. "I'm very happy I did it the way I did it," she said. "I don't know what motivated me. But I did it through a shift in my mental state. I convinced myself that alcohol was poisonous, which it is, and that I didn't want it anymore."

Lorraine supplemented this mental shift with hypnosis tapes, prayer, and books. But ultimately, quitting drinking was an internal act for her, a choice that she made and that she has succeeded in maintaining. "Six months after quitting, I just did not want to drink anymore. I tried to take one drink just to test it and it made me ill. Knock on wood, I haven't wanted one since."

Of course, addiction is an illness of its own, and it can happen to people of all personality types and for a variety of different reasons. But I hope that you can learn two important things from Lorraine's struggle with addiction. First of all, if you're shy, it's possible that the "community-support" approach to a problem (no matter what that problem is) is not best. Like Lorraine, support groups might cause you more stress than peace. If that's the case, you might be better off seeking a more individualistic approach such as Lorraine's mind-set shift, hypnosis, and books that can provide advice and support, or individual therapy.

Second, being different from the crowd is okay! If you're shy you may feel insecure in large groups, but you probably have a great deal more inner strength than you realize. Think about it this way: Many people spend time in groups because they are afraid to be alone. Solitude can be a sign of inner strength. You can draw on that strength to help resolve even the most difficult challenges.

A Solitary Life

Leaving her job at a big law firm back in the nineties was the best thing that Lorraine ever did. "I was very happy," she remembered. But there were difficulties. "The only problem is it's very isolating. It's hard to get out and meet people, especially if you're already inclined to be introverted."

Loneliness can be a devastating problem for many people, particularly if you are shy and tend to spend a lot of time alone. In one scientific article that explored the subject of loneliness, the author announced that it "has been agreed that loneliness is a painful or unpleasant experience."[8]

We don't need psychiatric researchers to tell us that. Philosophers have been struggling with the loneliness of the human experience for millennia—since, I imagine, Pandora let it out of her *pithos* (jar) along with all the other evils of the world. Since then, there have been entire genres of music and poetry dedicated to the subject. I think Mother Teresa spoke with as much clarity and concision as any scholarly writer when she said, "The most terrible poverty is loneliness, and the feeling of being unloved." Sadly, according to a recent study, as many as 20 percent of all Americans report feeling lonely.[9]

The scientific article made two other very important points. The first is that loneliness is a feeling, not an objective truth—or as they put it, "People can feel lonely in the company of many others or be alone without feeling lonely."[10] Doesn't that ring true? Have you ever had the alienating experience of being with a group of people but not feeling "connected"; or conversely, being in the flow of a great individual project and not aware at all of being alone?

This gets us to the second important point in the article: "Almost uniformly, a distinction has been made between loneliness and aloneness."

I couldn't agree more. There is an immense difference between loneliness and aloneness. Loneliness is a feeling of sadness that we can experience even in the company of our dearest friends or lovers. As the Harry Nilsson song "One" (famously covered by Three Dog Night) goes, "Two can be as bad as one / It's the loneliest number since the number one."

Aloneness, on the other hand, or solitude can be a sign of great strength and a positive experience. This is something that I know a thing or two about. I have ridden a bike and a motorcycle across the country, sailed all over the Gulf of Mexico and the Caribbean Sea, and kayaked some of America's most beautiful rivers—all by myself. I take great pleasure in the opportunity for self-reflection that solitude allows, and in the way that these solo adventures test my strength as an individual. And interestingly, the other solo adventurers I met on these trips were some of the most outgoing people you can imagine. We often think of people who are alone as being weak—too scared to go out and make friends—but in fact, people who spend time alone often have a great deal of inner strength.

The challenge is learning to accept your own solitary personality and being comfortable saying to the world, "Yes, I spend time alone—and that's a good thing."

Lorraine, for example, holds a few relationships—her family members and some special friends—very close. She doesn't need or want the vast network of friends that some of us desire. But she spent many years thinking that she *should* want to be part of a huge social network, should want to feel like getting out and about and should join more clubs and groups. Then she felt inadequate because she wasn't doing so.

This is a struggle that Caroline Knapp also deals with in her article about shyness. Spurred on by her frustration with her own shyness and her feelings of inadequacy, Knapp goes on a campaign to make her neighbors like her—by chatting with them over the fence, and eventually even bringing them a pie. One day she is rewarded for her efforts when one of her neighbors, Frank, stops by her house to invite her for dinner. Taking a deep breath, Knapp forces herself to accept the invitation and goes so far as to set a date.

> I felt brave and confident, fully aware that I'd done the noble thing, that I'd cast a vote for risk and sociability instead of fear and solitude, and that on the day in question.... I'd come down with a horrible, debilitating case of the flu.[11]

And that is exactly how she eventually escapes the engagement. Knapp's story perfectly expresses the balance between social expectations and strength from within in the life of a shy person. As a good-hearted person, she wants to be friendly with her neighbors. She just doesn't want a raft of semistrangers as new friends.

In fact, when it comes to relationships, shy people tend to pour their attention into the few people they *do* let into their life. And their incredible sensitivity to social situations makes them quite empathic and supportive: Shy people are really good friends to have.

If you don't believe me, read Gail Caldwell's book *Let's Take the Long Way Home,* about her relationship with Caroline Knapp, who died of lung cancer in 2002. It's a very powerful portrait of a friendship.

A Shy Companionship

But how does a shy person go about making those few special friends, or meeting a loved one? Traditional social arenas such as bars, clubs, or organized groups are often anxiety provoking and can cause a shy person to shut down.

But there are ways around that. Some types of group activities are designed to encourage people to be alone together—to exist in solitude, with no pressure or confinement—while in the company of others. Meditation and yoga are two practices that permit this kind of socializing, and Lorraine has recently begun participating in both. It's a good way to go out and meet people without becoming overwhelmed.

The Internet has also begun to open doors to people who don't enjoy social situations. Text messaging is a whole new opportunity for people who want to build relationships without participating in the events on which relationships are commonly built. In fact, one study of college students found that although there are many reasons to text (ease of communication is a big one, as is procrastination), shy students tend to use it to help alleviate loneliness, without giving up their right to be alone.[12]

The Internet is also becoming increasingly important as a dating opportunity for everyone—including shy people. Lorraine delights me by sending regular updates of her adventures with online dating. (She's got a great sense of humor about it.)

I'm glad to say that as I write this chapter, Lorraine is currently dating someone whom she met on an Internet dating site, and whom she refers to affectionately as "sort of a very strange bird, like I am." Wouldn't surprise me at all to hear about engagement plans soon.

Lorraine tells me that being with someone who shares her personality type is a good thing. She prefers being with someone who's quiet, because there's no pressure to go out and party (although at fifty-two, she says with a laugh, she's pretty much past the partying age). About the man she's currently dating, she says, "It's good because we encourage each other to get out and do things. And that's been very nice."

Plus, as an observer and interpreter of society, Lorraine can put her skills to use to inform and entertain the rest of us. She's writing a humor book about dating.

CONCLUSION: ARE YOU SHY?

Where do you fall on the social anxiety continuum? Are you extroverted? Independent? Have you found ways to use your shyness to your advantage? Or do you still struggle against your own natural instincts?

Allow yourself to think back to the past month. How many times did you find yourself in a social situation that made you uncomfortable? One time? Two times? Once a week? Once a day? If you notice a pattern of discomfort in your own life, ask yourself this serious question: *Do I need to be participating in these activities?*

"Need" is a funny word. Society says that you need to "go out" every Friday and Saturday night. Your boss might say that you need to attend networking events. Your friends might say you need a spouse. But when you break it down, you'll see that society is really saying you need to unwind *in the way that suits you best* during the weekends. Your boss is saying that you need to perform well at your job. Your friends are saying that they don't want you to feel lonely.

Only you can decide whether a social solution is the best way to meet your needs. If you're shy, the truth is that it's probably not.

If your dominant trait is shyness, there are so many things you can do to embrace your trait. First of all, if you're beating yourself up because you don't like big social situations—stop! You are lucky to be so confident and independent, and you can go ahead and take advantage of that trait. Make time to do the things you really love to do—whether it's working in your garden, dancing to loud music in your empty kitchen, or just curling up with a good book. Think about taking on some projects that you can do by yourself. And if you do want to incorporate more people into your life, find ways to do it that don't force you into uncomfortable situations.

There's no reason why your dominant trait should cause you un-happiness. If you embrace your trait, you'll find that it comes with so many ascendant strengths—such as sensitivity, independence, and productive solitude. If you use these to your advantage, I think you will find that you are living a happier and more productive life.

FIVE hyper-alert GENERALIZED ANXIETY DISORDER

I THINK a lot of people are going to recognize themselves in this trait.

Few among us have escaped the sometimes paralyzing effects of being hyper-alert—of having some degree of anxiety. At one time or another, most of us experience moments when we're deeply worried about one or more aspects of our lives. I like to think of anxiety as a smoke detector—the alert system—that is built into our brains. We all know the rush of adrenaline that occurs when it looks as if you might be heading for a car accident. The sudden surge of energy allows you to heighten your reaction time and propels you to take rapid, lifesaving actions. In similar ways, anxiety often represents an early warning sign that something is amiss in your life and needs to be addressed. In healthy proportions, anxiety keeps us alert and on our toes when we sense threats to ourselves, and it can motivate us to behave in positive, often highly constructive ways.

My friend Leonard is a good example of someone whose "smoke alarm" was going off, and it ultimately helped him make important changes in his life. Leonard is a hardworking, pretty tightly wound guy. He has been this way for as long as he can remember. "I always wanted to do well," he said. "I still remember college. On Friday nights a lot of kids would go drinking and partying, having a good time. I would go to the library and work. I was worried that if I didn't keep up with my homework, my reading, write my papers, and prepare for exams, then I wouldn't perform at the top." Leonard suffered a lot of headaches from the stress. After graduation, these got even worse as he started to climb the corporate ladder.

One day, on his way to work, Leonard had a panic attack on the subway. There was no specific trigger. He thought he was having a heart attack. "Your temples sweat and your heart starts beating really fast," he recalled. "It's hard to breathe. You feel dizzy. You think you're about to pass out. And you might just die right there and then." He had a second attack in his office. After each one, Leonard went to see his cardiologist, who gave him a battery of tests. "I was fine," Leonard said, at least according to the test results. But he wasn't fine—and his inner alert system was letting him know.

Leonard is a person who is very much on alert. But, as we will see, that is not necessarily a bad thing. Panic attacks represent a ten-plus on the anxiety continuum and are certainly not healthy, but the right amount of heightened awareness can be a good thing.

THE CONTINUUM MODEL: HYPER-ALERTNESS

GENERALIZED ANXIETY CONTINUUM				
COMPLACENCY		ENERGY		ANXIETY
0	3	5	7	10+
Absent		Dominant		Superdominant

Anxiety—that state of being on alert—is essentially an unusual, unnatural, heightened sense of apprehension over something in the future that may or may not happen. The worst form of anxiety is when you worry about something that is outside your control; or you worry about all kinds of possible events that have a very low likelihood of occurring, or you worry that you worry too much. So, for example, someone will worry about a friend's choice of a career. *How could she consider that profession? It will be horrible for her. She can't possibly think that would be the right thing to do!* Another person might be morbidly afraid of a pandemic flu that's supposedly going to wipe out half the population. *What will life be like after that disaster?* He or she will ruminate and fret and think of a hundred different outcomes, all of them bad.

On the other hand, if you have little or no anxiety in your life, you are complacent and calm. People like this live according to a mantra that goes something like, *No worries, mon.* They don't react too much to stressful circumstances, and they have the ability to remain emotionally disconnected. This can be helpful, for example, when faced with making unpleasant or unpopular decisions. But if you're *too* relaxed and calm and not aggressive enough, you might miss important opportunities, put dilemmas on the back burner, or stay in dead-end relationships or jobs for years. Lack of anxiety may give you a false sense of security too. A person at this end of the continuum might talk to strangers without consideration for her own personal safety; sign contracts without reading every sentence; not be adequately insured; be unconcerned about monetary reserves; blow off medical appointments. These people are great targets for unscrupulous wheeler-dealers. They don't bother looking at the hidden underbelly of things.

Anxiety at the opposite end of the spectrum is also a problem. It can take on a life of its own. For people who are constantly worried, nervous, and anxious about everything, anxiety essentially defines their personality. Their anxiety mechanism—the smoke alarm—is out of whack, which leaves them in a state of heightened anxiety, even near panic, a great deal of the time. At the extreme end of the continuum, when you reach a nine or a ten, severe anxiety can balloon into full-blown depression if left unchecked and untreated. In fact, as I've said before, depression almost always accompanies all of the traits when a person reaches a nine or ten on the continuum. But the link between anxiety and depression is particularly strong—at least half of all people who live with an anxiety disorder will experience a major depressive episode during their lives[1]—and numerous studies are now investigating the connection between the two. In my clinical experience, nearly everyone with severe anxiety also experiences depression.

There is no better portrayer of intense anxiety than Woody Allen, who has made a career of embodying neurotic characters in his films. But while his (and his characters') anxiety can be overwhelming, the comedian doesn't exemplify the severe anxiety I've just discussed. He's more like a seven or an eight on the continuum. In his classic 1986 film *Hannah and Her Sisters,* Allen goes through a period of anxiety when a doctor orders a CAT scan after observing an unusual spot in his brain. He walks out of the doctor's office, hands jammed into his coat pocket. "Okay," he tells himself. "Keep calm. You're going to be okay. Don't panic."

And then, in the next shot: "I'm dying, I'm dying, I know it, there's a spot in my lungs!... There's a tumor in my head the size of a basketball!"

Woody Allen's panic attacks and neuroses are the trademarks of his acting career. But in real life, overwhelming anxiety can be debilitating. Many a mother, for example, frets about her kids and sometimes the worries can get out of control. She finds herself imagining that the worst has happened every time the kids are a few minutes late, or the phone rings late at night, or she hears a siren in the distance. The worry can turn into physical panic. Her heart races and she feels as if she can't breathe.

With some patients, the anxiety has taken on a life of its own by the time they come to see me. Many people, especially those who are ten-plus on the generalized anxiety continuum, find that the biggest source of anxiety is actually the anxiety itself. They think that worrying all the time is abnormal, and so they can't stop worrying about worrying. Wow.

Consider this simple question for yourself: Does anxiety prevent you from living your life the way you want to live it? If so, you're far enough along in the continuum to consider getting professional help.

Healthy and controllable anxiety, being hyper-alert, on the other hand, enables you to think about things that could happen, put a smart plan in place to deal with those things if they do in fact come about—and then put the matter to rest.

And if you're called upon to act in a stressful situation, anxiety can be one of our strongest resources. That rush of adrenaline, instead of being paralyzing, can give us heaps of courage. It provides us with the needed energy, awareness, and confidence to do what we need to do in life's toughest moments.

REDEFINING GENERALIZED ANXIETY DISORDER

"Anxiety" is such a common word that many people don't even realize it can actually be classified as a mental disorder. In fact, the DSM-IV lists eight different kinds of anxiety disorders including panic disorders, phobic disorders, and even OCD. The lines between these different disorders can be blurry and most people with anxiety have more than one. But within the limitations of the DSM, generalized anxiety disorder (GAD) is the category that best describes the far end of the anxiety continuum.

People who have GAD suffer from excessive, uncontrollable anxiety and worry. This anxiety makes them feel irritable and tense, unable to sleep, easily fatigued, and restless. It is so all-consuming that it causes significant distress or impairment in the person's daily life. Folks with GAD are unable to go to work, to take care of their kids, to get out of bed—all because of their overwhelming anxiety.

Sometimes this anxiety can become so consuming that it can lead to depression. Anxious people may become so anxious they cannot function, and that loss of functionality, along with crippling anxiety, can make people depressed. I think of depression as falling at the outer edges of the anxiety continuum. It's the least desirable outcome of superdominant anxiety. The good news, though, is that treating anxiety can get a person back up and running, and help reduce depression to manageable levels.

But just a little further down the continuum, your smoke alarm system can also propel you to work in purposeful and positive ways toward living a better life.

Leonard, for example, viewed his panic attacks as his body sending strong signals that he was not in a good place in his life psychologically or spiritually. He responded by quitting his corporate job and embarking on a new career. Luckily, some people in his office had ties to the entertainment industry, and Leonard discovered in working with them that he loved dealing with "talent."

Now Leonard works behind the scenes in the entertainment industry. He is a self-confident guy and he uses his energy, enthusiasm, and charisma to promote his celebrity clients. Just as important as his self-confidence and personal charm, Leonard sees his worrying—yes, worrying, no longer anxiety—as a trait that helps him be very successful.

"What would happen," he asked me one day, "if my client is working on a film and a movie very similar to his comes out before he finishes with his? How would we handle that? How can I make sure I stay on top of competing projects? If I do learn about a similar project, what's the best way for me to let my client know?"

By thinking ahead, anticipating problems, and being vigilant on behalf of his clients, Leonard stays on top of his game. "I think the fact that I tend to be what people might call, colloquially, a 'worrier' is a good thing," he said. "It actually serves me well in this profession, because if I were resting on my laurels, or just assuming that everything would always go well, I don't think I would be successful in this job."

Science backs up what Leonard has figured out for himself. In 2008, a team of psychologists at Stanford University did a study to find out whether anxiety could be good for us. In the first half of the study, they tested people's anxiety levels. To do this, they scanned the brains of healthy adults and instructed them to think about the possibility of losing money. The scans revealed that some people, when considering financial loss, showed greater than normal activation of an area of the brain known as the anterior insula—an area that is associated with anxiety.[2]

Months later, the same participants were invited to return to the lab. They were asked to play a game and received coaching on how to avoid losing. The naturally anxious people—the ones whose brain scans had shown higher activation levels in the anterior insula—proved to be better able to learn how to avoid loss in this game. Those subjects who had not shown heightened levels of activation in that brain area had a more difficult time learning how to avoid loss. As a result, they lost more money.

What does this mean? In this case, the study suggests that people who tend to be more anxious about money are better able to learn skills that will help prevent financial loss. The anxiety works to their advantage. A little anxiety, in this case, can go a long way—not only with money but with all areas of life as well.

An Evolutionary Imperative

Anxiety has been around for thousands of years. According to evolutionary psychologists, it is adaptive to the extent that it helped our ancestors avoid situations in which the margin of error between life and death was slim. Anxiety warned people when their lives were in danger: not only from saber-toothed tigers, cave bears, hungry hyenas, and other animals stalking the landscape, but also from adversarial, competing tribes. Being on alert helped ancient people fight predators, flee from enemies, or "freeze," blending in, as if camouflaged, so they wouldn't be noticed. It mobilized them to react to real threats to their survival. It pushed them into keeping their children out of harm's way. Anxiety thus persisted through evolution in a majority of the population because it was (and can be) an advantageous, life-saving trait.

Nowadays, the threat from saber-tooth tigers is pretty close to zero (unless you count the person two cubes over who always has a snarl on his face!), but we react the same way to modern threats to our well-being: demanding bosses, wayward kids, overbusy lives, or the unrelenting economic uncertainty of recent times. The responses we associate with anxiety—rapid heartbeat, quick breathing, and pounding blood flow—are still the body's way of gearing up for stressful situations. We have millions of years of evolutionary anxiety hardwired into our brains to alert and mobilize us.

This gearing-up mechanism helps explain why one of the most common complaints associated with anxiety is sleeplessness. "If there was something I would change about my life," an otherwise self-content Leonard told me, "I would be a better sleeper." He thinks that our whole hyped-up culture contributes to this problem. "We're all so overextended that by the time you try to go to sleep, it's almost time to get up. Everyone is pressured by the onslaught of new technologies, and expectations of other people, and just how hard they need to work to achieve what their parents or grandparents did."

That is a *lot* of worrying. No wonder so many hyper-alert types turn to alcohol and other sedating medications to take the edge off.

Hyper-Alertness and Meds

I recently received the following inquiry on my website from Robert, who has experienced anxiety of mysterious origin all his life:

> I suffer from what I have always called butterflies in my stomach and anxiety. These feelings have been with me since I was a young boy, and I am now forty-four years old.
>
> There are no reasons for me to worry; it just seems that I am predisposed to worry. When I was younger I used to drink alcohol. I no longer do this, but as I age and think back to those times, I have come to realize that after two drinks my butterflies disappeared and I felt much calmer, with a clearer mind, experienced slower thought patterns, and was more self-assured. As I have aged, after some extensive periods of anxiety I would start to feel down and depressed.
>
> I have seen doctors and they have prescribed SSRIs [antidepressants] to deal with my anxiety. These work, but then I feel quite sluggish. I only take half a tablet.
>
> Can you tell me what hormones/chemicals are causing me to feel so anxious? Are there any blood tests that I can undergo to see if I have an excessive or limited amount of hormones in my blood? Could my thyroid glands possibly be out of whack? Could it be that my adrenal gland is causing this?

I told Robert that there are indeed many medical conditions that might cause anxiety. Chronic heart disease, obesity, thyroid dysfunction, irritable bowel syndrome, fibromyalgia, chronic pain, cancer—the list goes on and on. As far as the adrenal glands, they are quite important when dealing with anxiety. They are involved with both mental and physical stress on the body. Stimulants such as caffeine cause the adrenal glands to activate, while a vitamin deficiency can cause them to be sluggish. Virtually any type of physical or mental stress can affect the adrenals. And yes, hormones can be a definite cause, and men can suffer tremendously from hormone imbalances just as women can.

The point is that numerous medical diagnoses can have anxiety as a symptom. So first get a detailed medical history and blood work performed by your doctor. Any medical causes, if present, could be addressed at that time.

If you get the all-clear from your physician after a medical checkup, then you must do more work to identify the root cause of your anxiety. As I've said, anxiety *often* represents an early warning sign that something is amiss in your life and needs to be addressed. The first thing I have my patients do is to take a full personal inventory: What are you feeling about your family, spouse, friends, job, and other fundamental elements of your life? This anxiety may be the result of subjective, internal conflicts that might not be consciously apparent to you. However, introspection usually can bring these to the surface.

If you find some underlying conflicts, then you can work to address them one at a time. You'll be amazed at how taking control can have a calming effect. However, if nothing concrete comes up in your personal inventory and the symptoms keep getting worse and start interfering with how you wish to lead your life, then it may well mean that medications are indicated and a psychiatric evaluation is called for.

A note of caution: Alcohol is a depressant that slows down brain activity, so when you drink, you naturally experience slower thought patterns and calmness, as Robert reported. That, however, is never a good option to combat chronic anxiety because it takes more and more alcohol over time to have the same effect, and this leads to addiction. We'll see in the following chapters how other of the traits besides anxiety can lead to struggles with addiction, but also how you can find within the trait itself the strength to overcome it.

For example, twenty-eight-year-old Alexis, the event planner we met in chapter 3, started to take anti-anxiety medication after her parents got divorced. But she is very health-conscious (as anxious people often are), and found that she didn't like how the meds fit in to her life. "If I don't desperately need them then I'd rather not go there," she said. And, as we'll see, she's doing just fine without them—by facing and embracing who she really is.

Ascendant Strengths

So some degree of anxiety is healthy and can be advantageous to you. Being hyper-alert confers the following ascendant strengths:

VIGILANCE Alert people often pay close attention to people, events, and situations, anticipating future hazards or weighing the alternatives of a course of action, leaving nothing to chance. Their vigilance helps them focus on the quality of their work. They also tend to be careful about personal health—watching what they eat, monitoring their weight, keeping tabs on blood pressure and cholesterol, and having regular checkups with their doctors.

PREPAREDNESS I was a Boy Scout—and I still adhere to the Scout credo "Be prepared," particularly after living through the devastating one-two punch of Hurricanes Rita and Katrina in 2005. The same preparedness that steels you against natural disasters and other dangers can also be used to maximize opportunities. People with this strength excel at job interviews, schoolwork, athletics, competitions, public speaking, and many other areas. Some of the best public speakers I know admit to incredible anxiety before each talk. They are able to turn that anxiety into an empowering energy when they speak.

INTUITION Intuition is an internal radar of wisdom and guidance. I sometimes call it "knowing without knowing how you know." People who leverage their anxiety productively tend to have a sharp sense of what could happen. They "follow their gut" and are good at spotting what's going to be a problem tomorrow—and planning around it.

OBSERVATION Talent for observation is well developed in people who tend to be anxious. Why? Because they're highly aware of their surroundings. Such people can notice even subtle changes in their environment and can put their powers of observation to good use in such fields as research, law enforcement, art, or photography.

LIFE WITH A SMOKE ALARM

Paying attention to your anxiety, rather than trying to ignore these feelings, is important and helpful. Researchers have found that the incidence of illness increases in people who suppress their emotions, particularly anxiety. What's more, your anxiety-backed hunches can be right! Remember, alertness is the smoke alarm of life.

I have a high-strung friend, Sue, whose kids were going on a school field trip by chartered bus. Sue drove her kids to school and walked with them to the waiting bus. She met the bus driver, who seemed nice enough, and watched as her kids climbed aboard. Suddenly, she felt an overwhelming sense of concern. She hesitated for a moment, then heeded her feeling. She told the driver that she had decided to drive her kids to the event and shepherded them off the bus. On the way to the event, the bus was in an accident. Fortunately, no one was seriously injured. The driver admitted that he was dealing with some serious personal issues and was distracted at the wheel. Sue credits her inner voice for warning her of potential danger.

If you get a feeling like that, be sure to pay attention to it. Even if you're in the middle of a stressful day, take a time-out. Think about whether you've had the feeling before, and when, and what the situation was. Did you focus on the feeling the last time it hit? If not, what happened? Would paying attention have made a difference? Is there a pattern you can detect?

If, on the other hand, you find yourself overly on alert, take positive steps to take it down a notch on the anxiety continuum. As Leonard concluded, "I am self-aware in terms of this trait in my life. I try harder to get a lot of exercise, eat healthily, and take breaks. I work hard, but I also try to play hard. I have fun with my kids. And I'll just take breaks and do things that are fun, like watch *Mad Men,* or go to the movies, or take a walk along the river." And yoga. Leonard resisted it because he thought of it as a cliché. "But," he noticed, "just the act of yoga seems to disengage a certain amount of anxiety."

Aim to turn down the volume of your smoke alarm sometimes, but don't try to live entirely without it. It's important to listen to that anxious voice in your head to a healthy degree—and let anxiety work *for* you.

Work and Hyper-Alertness

"Anxiety gets a lot of bad press," began an article in *Science Daily.* It's true. And if I put the words "anxiety" and "work" together, you might think about some nasty outcomes, such as Leonard's panic attacks. "The accumulation of pressure and worry can build inside a person's body," he said. "So much of what we experience psychologically and emotionally becomes physical." Leonard compared anxiety to a metastasis of cancer cells that invades the entire body. Still, we have seen how some worrying also makes Leonard good at his job—once he found the right career match for his personality trait.

The same is true for Alexis, whose work as an independent event planner for a major museum on the East Coast is, as she describes it, "very intense." She must organize and stage events that will bring together groups of wealthy, sophisticated people for a few hours and satisfy their refined tastes in wining and dining. All the dishes are made entirely from scratch and every menu must be different from every other. Before each event her clients review her proposed plates and apply their exceptionally high standards to her work. How are the sauces? Are the ingredients locally sourced? Are the greens just right?

Alexis thrives on this process and her hyper-alertness works for her. "I'm always double-checking, rechecking, triple-checking," she said. She has had great success and takes enormous pride in her work. "If I found it debilitating I wouldn't be in the line of work I'm in. I think I would find a much less stressful job, something a little less intense, a little less demanding," she said.

Still, it's not all easy sailing. Like Leonard, Alexis suffers from sleeping problems. "The biggest way that anxiety manifests itself for me is not being able to sleep at night," she told me. "I often get so wrapped up in my job and wound up with whatever is happening that I can't sleep at all. I will lie in bed and look at the ceiling all night long." She tempers this unpleasant side effect of her anxiety by engaging in an exercise program six days a week. She's strict about keeping to her routine. "If I don't do it, I just feel *off* for the rest of the day. I can't *not* do it." Hers is basically a logical and healthy response to an anxiety situation, and I applaud that.

Relationships and Hyper-Alertness

Sometimes hyper-alert and worrying people will be attracted to other people with a similar personality profile (although again, when it comes to *romantic* relationships, the general rule of thumb is that high scores on a trait tend to do better with lower scores on that same trait). Leonard, for example, is drawn to "people who tend to feel deeply and worry more than I do." This has the interesting effect of turning him—the worrier—into the rock in his friendships. "People tend to turn to me for guidance and comfort, a sense that everything is okay, that things are going to go well, for optimism." Think about it. Leonard is a worrier, but "those qualities help me watch out for people," he said. His anxiety actually helps him have a calming effect on other people who are more anxious.

For Alexis, on the other hand, "When I meet somebody with similar tendencies to mine, it usually doesn't work. I've found that 'opposites attract' works better—with me being more of the high-strung person and the other person being more low key and not as tightly wound."

Her last long-term relationship was with a person she described as "incredibly ADHD," while she thinks of herself as "the polar opposite of ADHD." (Notice how these diagnostic categories are so imbued in the culture that we go about casually diagnosing others—and ourselves.)

The yin and the yang of that relationship worked well for Alexis. "I'm always the one that's the driving force. Where are we going to have dinner? What are we going to do this weekend? What are we going to do this summer? What are we going to do for the holidays?" Her boyfriend helped her to relax. "He'd say, all right, let's tackle one thing at a time. Why don't we figure out what we're going to do over the holidays because they come first. We don't need to stress out about next summer yet."

With a dose of humor, Alexis drew me a picture of what a relationship with another anxious person like herself might look like: "I think if I was with somebody exactly like me—yes, what *are* we going to do next summer?—we would both spin off the face of the earth together, freaking out and in a tizzy about everything."

This reminds me of the Tasmanian Devil from the old Looney Tunes cartoons. Alexis's idea of spinning into an unproductive freak-out is pretty much the equivalent of worrying about whether the next time you step outside you're going to get hit by a meteor shower. The key is to turn your hyper-alert energy into something that gives you awareness and confidence about what to do in life's trying situations. And to start to think more positively and proactively about those situations. Ask yourself the question, "What is the worst thing that could happen?" Could you survive that thing if you really, really had to? The answer is usually yes, you could survive, the rest is just details. People tend to rise to the challenges in life and become stronger in the process.

CONCLUSION: ARE YOU HYPER-ALERT?

Most of us think of anxiety as something that we need to keep under control. *I'm so anxious,* we think. *I need to calm down.* But if anxiety is your dominant trait, you can actually put that nervous energy to good use. You may find that you perform best under high-pressure scenarios, or that you get a thrill every time you approach a deadline.

In the Stone Age, hyper-alert people helped protect villages from life-threatening risks. There's no reason why the preparedness that comes with this personality trait can't be similarly advantageous today. While it's important not to let anxiety consume you, you can allow yourself to thrive off this aspect of your personality. You can change your schedule so that you work close to deadlines.

You can enter a competition, whether it's chess or a triathlon. You can volunteer to organize a hike or another event—your anxiety will help you manage the many moving parts. Anxiety carries ascendant strengths including preparedness, intuition, and observation. As a hyper-alert person, you can put these traits to good use when you embrace your trait.

six dramatic HISTRIONIC

"*Life is being* on the wire," said Karl "Papa" Wallenda, the dare-devil tightrope walker. "Everything else is just waiting."

Papa Wallenda was being literal. He lived for the time he spent in the limelight, the attention of the crowds, and, yes, the thrill of the performance.

We can also take Papa Wallenda's words as symbolic, a rallying call for dramatic personalities. For dramatic people, life is a performance. When you walk into a room, people take notice. At work, you are the linchpin that holds a group together, and its public face. In your personal life, you are emotionally vulnerable and also emotionally dramatic: Sometimes your life can feel like a roller coaster, or a tightrope performance!

I'm a seven on the dramatic personality continuum these days. Like Papa Wallenda, I love to perform—though in my case, it's my work in TV, radio, and the Internet that brings me to life. I love my career as a clinical psychiatrist, and I take great meaning from the work I do with my patients. But the first time I stood in front of the camera, way back in 1987, was one of those "aha" moments. *Wow. I love this.* I love being on camera and talking about mental health. I love being the expert and discussing human behavior. I love people calling and asking for advice. I love feeling like I'm doing a good thing, and making a difference not only one patient at a time, but also by reaching thousands of folks all at once through the media.

After that first experience on television, I was hooked.

Lots of performers are dramatic: Elton John, Tom Cruise, Lady Gaga, and Beyoncé, to name a few. In fact, "dramatic personality" is so synonymous with performers that it has worked its way into the English language. Take the word "diva." It comes from the Latin for "goddess," and it originally referred to singers: The technical definition of "diva" is "distinguished female singer." But we all know what diva means in popular culture: fussy, demanding, the center of attention—on stage *and* off.

The word "histrionic" has similar roots. It means "theatrical or stagy" and it comes from *histrio,* which is the Greek word for "actor." Among psychiatrists, though, it refers to the disorder—histrionic personality disorder—that occupies the far end of the continuum for this trait. I hope that this book will help us reclaim the word "histrionic" as a celebratory adjective, not as a derogatory one.

While histrionic behavior is closely associated with actors, not everyone on the histrionic continuum is a professional performer. William, a prestigious lawyer, is a wonderful example. As a young man, he dreamed of going into theater. But, he said, "Everybody I knew, including people who were way more talented than I was, was working as a waiter in New York City. I didn't feel that was going to make for a happy life."

So William went into law, as his father and both of his grandfathers before him, with one major difference. While his father, a corporate lawyer, encouraged him to take the same path, William knew that he was destined for something different. "I was definitely clear that, if I was going to do law, I would be the actor," he said. William's love for the stage became integral to his litigation work. He even speaks of his closing arguments as a type of performance art: "My closing arguments were always done without notes. Sometimes I was accused of memorizing the whole thing. I'd say, 'I haven't memorized anything. I'm just telling you a story, but I'm really good at telling stories.'"

William is not a performer in the traditional sense. But he is a seven on the dramatic continuum.

The Continuum Model: Dramatic

HISTRIONIC CONTINUUM				
FLAT AFFECT		ENTERTAINING		HISTRIONIC
0	3	5	7	10+
Absent		Dominant		Superdominant

The dramatic trait can be thought of as flowing along a continuum ranging from showing very little emotion at all (a state known as *flat affect*) to histrionic personality disorder.

People with a flat affect don't feel or express their emotions much at all. They don't feel particularly sad when they experience tragedy or disappointment; they don't feel great joy when they experience good fortune. Furthermore, they rarely show what little emotion they might be feeling. These are people who attend funerals and shed no tears. Others get angry at them and they shrug it off. Bring them good news and it hardly seems to register. They are also often people we describe as unflappable—emotionally charged events don't disrupt the tasks they have at hand or derail them in the pursuit of their aspirations.

As you move further up the dramatic continuum, you begin to

show more emotional awareness. Your emotional state becomes an increasingly important part of your decision-making process. You seek out pleasure and, when you are in a situation that causes you pain, frustration, or sorrow, you express those feelings and you seek to change the circumstance. Most of us fall somewhere within this range.

But for some people, the emotional state overwhelms other interests. These people often seem as if they are on an emotional roller coaster. They easily show their feelings, and every time their emotional state changes, they tell the world about it.

When one of my researchers was looking for case studies for this chapter, she met a twenty-four-year-old opera singer named Leora. Hoping to find a lead, she asked Leora if she knew anyone who fit the characteristics of a dramatic personality. She did not expect Leora to identify herself as one! Leora instantly recognized her own personality in the *dramatic* traits, and she was thrilled to tell her story in more detail. (This should not have been a surprise: Dramatic personalities are often wonderful storytellers, and they love, love, love to talk about themselves.)

Leora is an interesting case of dramatic personality because her parents are both Zen Buddhist teachers. We hardly think of Zen as being associated with drama. But I think Leora would say that Zen is about embracing who you are—whatever that may be.

That's certainly the approach her parents took. Some of Leora's earliest and most vivid memories are of her mother's emotional outbursts. "Sometimes my mother would get upset about something," Leora recalled. "I would worry about her because she seemed fragile. I remember sitting down with my dad once and talking to him about that. He said, 'She pretends to be fragile sometimes, and she thinks that she is sometimes, but she's really one of the strongest people I know.'" He called Leora's mom a "tiger."

What Leora took away from this was that the ability to be as intense as her mom was—to feel things so deeply and to express them so openly—was powerful. "My mother wasn't fragile or weak. She was showing incredible courage to be present with whatever was happening," Leora said.

That's what I mean when I talk about embracing your histrionic trait.

Unfortunately, when Leora went away to college, she found herself in a far less welcoming environment than she had experienced at home, and her dramaticism got a little bit out of control. There were a variety of factors that contributed to making Leora's college experience a challenging one. "I was pretty depressed in my final year of college," Leora said. "I really didn't want to be there anymore." She felt academically burned out, and was also fed up with the social world of college and dorms. One problem was particularly nagging—there was no one left to meet or date. (Histrionics love to meet new people.) It was such a small school that by senior year, "if you hadn't dated a guy yourself yet, all of your friends already had."

These emotional challenges probably pushed Leora a bit further along the dramatic continuum and made her more unstable and sensitive than usual. Unfortunately, the world isn't always tolerant of behavior that is perceived as histrionic. People who don't have this trait often find dramatic personalities shallow or overwhelming.

This is something that I've heard before as well: that my tendency to feel things strongly and express myself in emotive ways is overwhelming, especially to those who don't know me well. I've always seen this self-expression as natural and authentic, and never really understood why it would make others uncomfortable. But other personality types handle their emotions in different ways. Shy people, for example, are more likely to take the time to think through and process their emotions before they express them.

They find it difficult to respond to a raw expression of emotion that can feel like a barrage.

Leora experienced this firsthand. At college, she would often have dinner with a girlfriend to talk about what was going on in their lives. "One evening toward the end of the fall semester," she said, "I was feeling particularly fragile. My friend looked at me and said, 'You look like you're about to cry.' Which, of course, made me start crying right there in the middle of the dining hall, which was awful and embarrassing." The friend patted Leora on the shoulder, said that she could see Leora was in pain, and suggested she might go to psych services to seek help. Good idea, you might say! But Leora did not see it that way. She felt put down and rejected by her friend's advice.

The following week, the friend invited another person to join them at their dinner, as if they needed a third party to act as an emotional buffer. The evening fell apart, Leora said. "I never really talked to my friend again."

What happened? Leora's dramatic personality made her extra sensitive to her friend's behavior. Her emotional expressiveness made her friend uncomfortable, and probably put a strain on the relationship. At the same time, Leora lost confidence in her dramatic self. "I got the message that I was too emotional," she said. "I took it to mean that I shouldn't show that part of myself to people that I cared about."

People with extremely dramatic personalities often struggle with this. Although our society loves observing dramatic personalities on TV, we are not always as comfortable with that level of emotionalism in our personal lives. But when a dramatic person tries to repress his or her personality, it only leads to frustration and unhappiness.

Later in this chapter, I will describe some ways that dramatic personalities can alleviate this frustration so they can maintain healthy and happy relationships with others while still being true to themselves. Leora, for example, found a way to channel her emotionalism into her music, which has made her a world-class performer, and to balance her friendships (and romantic relationships) more evenly. But she is more accepting of herself and will tell you upfront: "Yes, sometimes I can be 'too much' for others. But that's who I am."

At that stage in her life, Leora was probably an eight on the dramatic scale. She struggled with her personality trait, but it never seriously interfered with her ability to function in the world.

At the far end of the continuum is histrionic personality disorder, an uncommon but severe personality disorder.

Redefining Histrionic Personality Disorder (HPD)

Histrionic personality disorder is described in the DSM-IV as "a pervasive pattern of excessive emotionality and attention seeking."

We can see some of these "symptoms" a little bit in Leora's story. Crying in the dining hall could be seen as "excessive emotionality and attention seeking." Leora certainly felt like it was excessive—that's what made it so embarrassing for her.

But to understand the full reach of this personality disorder, I'd like to turn to the diarist, novelist, and short-story writer Anaïs Nin. She was posthumously "diagnosed" with HPD by the psychologist Angie A. Kehagia, whose careful examination of Nin's biography determined that Nin was almost certainly histrionic. Although posthumous diagnosis is often problematic, in this case I think Kehagia's conclusions are extremely convincing.

The gap between Leora's public tears and Anaïs Nin's emotionally destructive behavior is enormous. I want to clarify here that the behavior of most dramatic people is nowhere near that of Nin, whose stormy life included many extramarital affairs, a marriage with a bigamist, a constant need for attention in every aspect of her life, and incest with her father when she was an adult. She was certainly a ten-plus on the continuum.

Nin, like many people with HPD, came from an unstable family background. Like other personality disorders, HPD is generally thought to be more heavily influenced by "nurture" than by "nature." Nin's father was a moody composer and pianist who had many extramarital affairs, and physically and emotionally abused the children. He abandoned the family when Anaïs was eleven. (Leora's healthy family life may be one reason why she has always stayed on the positive side of the continuum.)

By the time she was an adult, Nin showed every one of the diagnostic symptoms of HPD. By looking at Nin's life, it's easy to see how these behaviors can become destructive to oneself and to others. Needing to be the center of attention, for example, is one diagnostic criterion for HPD, and Nin exhibited this one in excess. When she attended a party, she would always provide entertainment by reading from her latest work, showing off her Spanish dancing, or singing. She also showed an unhealthy dependence on the response of her audience. After the guests would leave, Nin would sit down to carefully record everybody's words of admiration in her diary. Anyone who didn't flatter and praise her was written off as rude and ignorant.[1]

Because histrionic types experience their emotions in an exaggerated way, they tend to overestimate the intimacy they really have with other people—another diagnostic criterion of HPD. For example, one of Nin's so-called friends recalled about her: "I was sort of 'father-mother-confessor' to her, for she'd reappear, sit on the floor—her head in my lap—and tell me sad things of herself.... She wanted so much to be close to me, but she never seemed real to me."[2] Nin's antics often struck people as unreal and inauthentic. As another friend recalled, she "needed so much, like an actress, to be in the limelight."[3]

The destructive extreme of Nin's personality is most clearly observed in the way she expressed herself sexually. One symptom of HPD is inappropriate sexual seduction or provocation. Not only was she seductive and provocative to people who might be considered "fair game," Nin also went out of her way to seduce people who were out-of-bounds, including two of her psychologists as well as her father. (She wrote about her desire to seduce her father in her diary, evidence that she was an active participant, and even initiator, in the affair.) While married to her first husband, Nin married a second time, without letting on that she was already spoken for.

By reading her diary (which she published, in true histrionic fashion), we can see how Nin's behavior was destructive not only to others but to herself. She was tortured by her desires, appetites, and behaviors. She was needy and often deeply unhappy. (Notice how depression is so often a symptom at the high end of the trait continuums.)

In later life, Nin seems to have found some balance. Angie Kehagia, the scholar whose work on Anaïs Nin informs much of this chapter, reports that at some point in her fifties, Nin began to depart from the histrionic personality type, so much so that she was able to find "interpersonal happiness and fulfillment." I don't imagine that Nin ever had a flat affect. But through a combination of effective therapy and, interestingly enough, the process of writing and publishing her diary, Nin was able to move to a healthier place on the histrionic continuum.

This is why Anaïs Nin's story is such a good case for the continuum model. What I see in her story is a troubled woman whose genetic predisposition (her father showed many similar traits) and troubled childhood led her to develop an unhealthy personality. But the line between health and disorder was always blurry, and Nin was finally able to be at peace with herself, and with others.

A Cultural Imperative

Many chapters in this book feature a section on the "evolutionary imperative," which describes why evolution and natural selection have favored disorders that seem to be debilitating in every way.

Personality disorders (histrionic and narcissistic personality disorders) are a little bit different. These disorders are thought of as "axis II" in the DSM-IV, meaning that their genetic basis and their chemical treatment have not yet been identified. I believe that it's only a matter of time before these aspects of the disorders are found—remember, genetics and neuroscience are still very new fields of study. Once that happens, I think the distinction between axis I disorders, considered "major psychiatric conditions," and axis II disorders, considered less severe, will be made null.

Furthermore, in the forthcoming DSM-V, the speculation is that these two traits (narcissistic and histrionic personality) will not be included. Although the new DSM is still under revision, as of this writing it seems that the category of personality disorders will be reorganized. Individuals will receive a general diagnosis of "personality disorder," modified by specific types and traits.

You might think that following the lead of the DSM, I would have removed these traits from my list. But the truth is that both disorders predate the DSM, and the field of psychiatry, by millennia. Narcissism can be traced back to Greek mythology! In my twenty years of clinical experience, I have worked with countless people for whom these traits were dominant.

Finally, I think that we live in an era in which histrionic and narcissistic types are coming to the fore. The forces of social networking and reality TV have rapidly expanded the histrionic universe to the point where anyone with a histrionic streak might end up on TV, letting it all hang out. Dramaticism and narcissism are increasingly being embraced in our culture.

I think you will recognize these traits in yourself, or in people that you know, just as I have. That's why I've included both traits in this book.

Because the genetic element of the personality disorders is un-clear (because nurture—that is, how you were raised—seems to be much stronger than nature—that is, genetics/DNA), there is not yet a great deal of scientific research regarding the evolution of per-sonality disorders. We can, however, look at the issue from a more anthropological perspective to see how society has benefited from histrionics for thousands of years.

Imagine yourself sitting in a circle around a fire in a Stone Age village. You're draped in an animal fur, with the remains of a wild boar strewn around you. In the middle of the circle stands a man. Maybe he is the village elder, the source of sacred wisdom and guidance. Maybe he is the village seer, who interprets the past and predicts the future. The man is telling a story of the great hunt for a woolly mammoth. The entire village listens, enraptured, as he describes in elaborate detail the mythic history of the great warrior's victory over the beast in the wilderness. In prehistoric times, the end of the day was a time for relaxation, for listening to a good story, forgetting for a moment the often brutal conditions of Stone Age life, and maybe learning something about culture and community.

Entertainers play a similar role today. We often forget why we celebrate great performers, compensate them so immensely, and give them so much of our time. The reason is that the pleasure that they bring to our lives is invaluable. Even today, a great perfor-mance, book, or movie allows us to escape for a bit no matter how troubled our lives may be. You can't really put a price on that.

Anthropologists have long identified storytellers as the central figures of tribal life. These figures are not merely entertainers, al-though in the days before TV they certainly played that role. They

are also the repositories of cultural knowledge. They are responsible for remembering the community's history and, by extension,
its identity. It's their job to pass that information on to the next
generation.

Philosophers, sociologists, and other observers and academics
agree on the essential role of the storyteller. The French philosopher Jean-Luc Nancy described storytelling as the most important
moment in the construction of a community. German philosopher
Walter Benjamin described the storyteller as the source of exter-
nal wisdom, of morality, and of truth. The French anthropologist
Claude Levi-Strauss saw storytelling as the passing down of the
universal truths that govern society. And the American mytholo-
gist Joseph Campbell studied the role of stories and storytellers
in forming cultural traditions that have lasted to this day. And of
course, Campbell himself was a talented storyteller: The storyteller
of a mythic, Stone Age time is alive today in people like him.

Sociologists and philosophers have identified what geneticists
have yet to find: an evolutionary imperative for histrionic personalities that dates from the Stone Age and continues to be relevant
today. But my faith is with science. Give them five to ten more
years, and I'm confident that the genetic markers will be in place to
back up these theories.

Ascendant Strengths

Dramaticism carries with it wonderful potential qualities. People
strong in the trait tend to be sensation oriented, demonstrative,
and affectionate. They have rich imaginations and tell entertaining
stories. If you tend toward dramaticism, your ascendant strengths
include the following:

PERSONAL CHARM AND CHARISMA You tend to be lively, enthusiastic, and flirtatious and enjoy excellent social skills.

APPROPRIATE ATTENTION TO APPEARANCE AND GROOMING You care about how you look, how you are dressed, and how you are groomed. You like clothes. You follow fashion. You have a personal style.

ABILITY TO ENTERTAIN You like to be the center of the action. You enjoy being noticed. You're happy when people are watching you. Such attention generally brings out the best in you. You can be witty, charming, and gregarious, and are often the most talked about personality in the workplace.

TENDENCY TOWARD EMOTIONAL DEMONSTRATIVENESS AND PHYSICAL AFFECTION Displaying this kind of sensitivity and tenderness can be a huge part of building a loving, successful relationship. This strength is vital in parenting too. Children who come from loving homes where emotion is outwardly expressed fare well. Not only do they feel a healthy sense of self-worth, they value others and it shows in their good social skills.

Living a Dramatic Life

Many great performers, across all traditions, are dramatic personalities. Dancers and opera singers, movie stars and actors have all found ways to channel their dramatic personality into their art. Their ability to be emotionally vulnerable is often what gives the edge of authenticity to a performance. And for dramatic personality types, the performance gives back by providing a chance for catharsis.

Drama as Performance Art

Here's more of Leora's story. She had always loved to sing: She sang a lot with her family and took voice lessons as a child. But it wasn't until she went to college and began to study classical voice that she found her calling as a performer. "I took one lesson and it was completely transformative," she said. "The teacher got me to use this voice that was so much bigger than anything that I'd experienced. It was totally radical, and I wanted more of that."

Leora had always preferred pop music and show tunes to opera and other classical forms of singing. Now she fell in love with the way that the singing of classical music made her *feel.* Only later did she began to fall in love with the music itself. Even with her appreciation for the music, it truly comes alive for her only when she feels a strong emotional connection to it. "The ability to feel that emotion and let it flow through me and pass out of me to the audience is essential." In fact, she can always tell when someone does not make an emotional connection with the music. The performance feels slightly fake to her.

Leora's most profound experience with dramatic performance occurred just after her senior year of college. She was in the process of organizing and preparing her song for a recital when she received some terrible news: A friend of hers had just died in a car accident. Leora made up her mind to dedicate the performance to the memory of her friend. Here's how she describes what happened when she came on stage to introduce the evening's program:

"When I started talking about my friend and made the dedication, I began to cry. I was horribly embarrassed." Fortunately, Leora had a few minutes to gather herself while the first performer sang her piece. Then it was Leora's turn. She began to sing, and found herself giving the performance of a lifetime.

"There's a quality of openness and vulnerability that's really necessary for singing," she said. "And not just emotionally, but physically as well. If you try to hold something back, the voice doesn't flow. You can sing okay, but it doesn't have that magical sparkle to it. When everything is totally released, then it's really easy to sing, even the hardest stuff. It still takes a lot of energy and a lot of concentration, but the voice just flows out easily and it feels so good."

Leora's ability to tap in to her most vulnerable self allowed her to reach a whole new level of artistry that evening. Her performance had the transformative quality that characterizes great classical singing.

What's more, Leora found that singing helped her work through her sorrow over her friend's death. "The grief of it was too big for any other form of expression," she said. "Everything else was just breaking down, but I could still go back and practice."

If you are a dramatic personality and you have experience performing, you might be familiar with the transformative power of performance. Leora used music to channel some of her grief and, I would guess, she was able to be healthier in other aspects of her life as well. By channeling those strong emotions into a healthy pursuit, many dramatic people are able to keep their personal lives more balanced and in control.

Relationships and Emotionalism

Because dramatic people are so closely in touch with their emotions, they are often drawn to others who have the same kind of emotional depth that they do.

This is certainly true of Leora. For many years she was convinced that like attracted like. She actively pursued relationships with people who were highly emotional, just as she was. "I've always been drawn to artsy guys who like to talk about intense and deep things," she said.

During one six-month period, Leora had three intensely emotional relationships with men who were every bit as dramatic as she was. The first one was deeply depressed, wildly in love, and totally committed to her. After their third date, he started working on a two-year plan for their relationship. That ended that. The second guy was also very intense. He and Leora would have tear-filled conversations for hours on end. But he had difficulty making decisions. That relationship too ran its course. The third man fell in love with Leora virtually at first sight, but Leora never felt as much passion for him as he did for her.

At the end of that six-month period, Leora came to the conclusion that "it's very easy to confuse intensity with intimacy. They feel so similar on the surface." Ultimately, Leora saw all three men as pretentious and insincere. They weren't willing, as Leora put it, to "do the sustained, quiet work of knowing yourself and of being in a relationship."

If I had known Leora during this time, I would have urged her to follow the age-old adage "Opposites attract." There isn't always space for more than one dramatic personality in the room. That's why dramatic people tend to do best when partnered with another who can help keep the relationship grounded.

Leora came to the same conclusion. Soon after she broke up with the third dramatic man, she met a person whom she saw as an opposite personality. "He was a scientist, very concrete and rational. He wanted to conquer his emotions. He felt that emotions got in the way," she said. "And yet he had the core of genuineness that I didn't find with other people."

This is a love story and it does have a happy ending, but it took a while to get there. Six months into their relationship the couple hit a rocky patch. Leora's boyfriend cheated on her and she broke up with him. What's interesting, however, is that Leora didn't completely abandon the guy even though they had broken up. Instead, she kept the dialogue going. "I made him talk to me about it," she said. "I was more angry than I've ever felt before and I showed him that anger. But I didn't try to do anything specific about it. It was a pretty radical experience for him. He could see that his actions resulted in all this anger and yet we were still talking."

Over the course of the next three months, the two slowly came to trust each other again. "He had never really understood how profound the impact of his actions would be on me," Leora explained. She learned that he had conducted affairs in his previous relationships as well. When his partner found out and confronted him, he would simply call it quits. Leora refused to allow him to do that. "I made him go through the grieving process with me in order to understand the betrayal and the anger of it, the insecurity and fear and vulnerability." She called up all of her emotionality—her tiger—and put it to work in the relationship. "I didn't let him disappear and let myself feel bad and then get over it," she said.

Not many people want to put this kind of work into a relationship—especially not at first. But clinical studies show that couples who demonstrate greater levels of strife at the outset of their relationships, and who stay committed to the process of direct emotional expression with each other, fare better than those who play the blame game.[4]

Leora and her boyfriend are committed to that process, and their shared work around emotions continues. "It was outside of his scope of understanding that his actions could have that kind of emotional effect on any person," Leora said. "The way that we initially worked through it, and the way we continue to deal with it, is a process of trying to understand the differences in the way that we see the world and interact with it."

It's a challenge, but Leora is thriving. "When a person seems similar to me, I don't have as much curiosity about who he really is. I assume there is common ground. But being with someone who's clearly so radically different, I can't assume anything about him. There's a lot of space to get to know him as a different person."

Perhaps the best part of their relationship is that Leora feels that her boyfriend accepts her dramatic personality. "He doesn't see my intensity and emotionalism as something challenging that he has to deal with. He sees it as an asset to our relationship." In my opinion, Leora is actually able to express emotions for her boyfriend that he would never be able to express himself, helping to make their relationship stronger.

I'd like to note that dramatic relationships often look different from other relationships. Many of Leora's friends were concerned to see the way she dealt with her boyfriend's cheating. In fact, many people think that all healthy relationships are emotionally stable. That runs against everything a dramatic person is!

Instead, research shows that couples who work through emotional challenges and are open with each other tend to fare better than those that never struggle. It reminds me of how William, the lawyer, describes his relationship of twenty-eight years: "It's the most challenging relationship I've ever watched anybody have," he says. "We are constantly bickering. It's challenging. But I've watched lots and lots of people around me divorce, break up, whatever, and we haven't. And I used to think they all had better relationships than we do. But I guess one of the things that we do have is communication. We do ultimately hear each other and speak our minds. And I think that's really key to having a successful relationship."

In the end, the capacity for emotional intensity and demonstrativeness can bring tremendous honesty and depth to human relationships. It allows us to mine the riches of our experiences and to share this knowledge with others.

Emotionalism at Work

I've talked about how dramatic personalities can make great performers. But if you are a dramatic personality, that doesn't mean you should drop everything and catch the first plane to L.A. There are many careers that benefit from a dramatic personality.

William, who uses his storytelling abilities and love of the spotlight to win court cases, has a second career that has also benefited from his dramatic identity. Several years ago, he started a small company working with couples who are unable to have children. Today that company is one of the top five in the nation, with thirty employees.

William is obviously a savvy businessman, and I'll return to his story in the chapter on self-focus. But what's interesting here is how much emotionalism William has to bring to his job. He works with people who are feeling extremely vulnerable, and his conversations with them tend to be very intimate. So a great deal of his job is earning people's trust by telling his own story, about the struggles and challenges that he and his partner faced when they decided to start a family.

The ability to earn people's trust can be extremely useful for dramatic personalities. Trust begets trust, and the natural ability that dramatic folks have for telling stories about themselves and exposing their feelings helps other people feel comfortable with them.

That's definitely a trait that I use in my work as a psychiatrist. Nothing helps a patient or a TV audience feel more at ease than a personal story that lets them know you understand exactly what the situation is.

And it's a trait that's useful in any business. Although some business theorists might argue that we should all become automatons, the truth is that we are human—and people who are able to tap in to that humanity are likely to be successful in the workplace.

Some research shows in fact that histrionics and colorful folks are positively correlated with true transformational leadership. This is a surprise to many people. The conventional wisdom is that narcissists are our most effective leaders. But narcissists tend to overreport their leadership capabilities in relation to others' reports about them. That's who they are, after all. This creates a methods problem for researchers and probably overinflates our ideas about how effective narcissists are in the workplace. In other words, they tell us they're great, and we—the general public and the scientists who study them—tend to believe them.

Instead, two recent studies found an elevated number of histrionics among CEOs and senior managers as compared with the general population.[5] Why? It's likely due to these qualities: desire to be the center of attention, flirtatiousness, charm, and the ability to form relationships. Basically, people enjoy being around these entertaining, sociable, and emotionally expressive people. They trust them—and earning trust is essential to successful leadership. Employees who enjoy their jobs and trust their employers are more likely to be committed, hardworking, and creative.

So science shows that dramatic personalities are often the best kind to guide us into innovative spaces and toward professional success.

Other professions that dramatic people excel in include sales, marketing, public relations, and other endeavors that put them in the public eye. William says that when he took a personality test as a teenager, he was told he should be a teacher. Teachers who can engage their students fully and authentically are often the most inspiring. Since dramatic types thrive on performance and often put their best foot forward when they're in the limelight, they do best at jobs that highlight this talent. Their winning ways allow us to see life not simply in muted tones, but in the full spectrum of color.

Conclusion: Are You Dramatic?

Almost everyone loves a dramatic personality. If you are high on the histrionic continuum, then you are the life of every party. You are a talented performer, self-confident and charismatic in public. And you are empathetic toward others and emotionally open with the people you love.

These are all positive traits. Histrionic personalities have been society's entertainers and repositories of knowledge for millennia. Whether you are bringing joy to an unhappy friend or entertaining a paying audience, you can put your dramatic personality to work today. And as a histrionic personality, you are fortunate to have one of the most valued traits in today's society. As our infatuation with TV indicates, America loves a histrionic personality. I encourage you to embrace your inner dramatic side as well.

self-focused NARCISSISTIC

IT'S EASY TO JUDGE the people we deem "narcissists" for being overly self-absorbed and for having a grandiose self-image. And it's fun to make fun of the self-promotional era of social networking. I'll talk about some more serious consequences of this trend later. But the fact is that those whose personalities tend toward the narcissistic—what I call "self-focused" personalities—have a wealth of positive characteristics. These people are goal oriented and ambitious. They are charismatic leaders and they inspire greatness in others. They are politicians and movie stars, writers and CEOs.

Jason is a seventeen-year-old member of the digital generation. He has a Facebook account and a Twitter feed. Fans and acquaintances can peruse his photos (1,333 on Facebook), check out his connections (4,270 friends), and stay up-to-date on the hourly progress of his daily life via his Tweets. He has just been accepted to a prestigious East Coast university where he will study law just as his father and his grandfather did. Though he's a teenager, Jason already shows the trait that his father—William, who we met in the previous chapter—in an interview called "lawyerism."

"I definitely see in him many of the qualities that make a good lawyer," William said. "He's bright, thoughtful, arrogant, opinionated, provocative. He likes to prove a point and create a struggle where one may not exist. I share many of those qualities."

Most of those traits are typical of self-focused individuals.

The challenge for the self-focused person is learning how to temper that grandiose sense of self with an ability to relate in a positive way with the people around them. They must find a way to balance their self-focus and tendency toward inward thinking with empathy and concern for others. If they can't achieve that balance, those around them may not be willing to accept their behavior. That's what my colleague Dietrich, a self-focused serial entrepreneur, came to understand. Even his closest family members found him difficult to deal with and accused him of being narcissistic at times.

But Dietrich's personality always remained within the realms of "healthy narcissism." He may have driven his family a little crazy, but he never reached the real extremes of the narcissistic continuum, which is where pathological narcissism lies. When it becomes pathological, this trait is diagnosed as narcissistic personality disorder (NPD), a disorder characterized by an overinflated sense of self and disregard for others.

But for most of us, a little bit of narcissism can go a long way.

The Continuum Model: Self-Focus

NARCISSISTIC CONTINUUM				
INSECURE		VISIONARY		NARCISSISTIC
0	3	5	7	10+
Absent		Dominant		Superdominant

I think of healthy narcissism as basically a healthy belief in yourself, in who you are, and in what you are able to accomplish.

If you're at the low end of the narcissistic continuum, you may be quite insecure. People who are a zero, one, or two on this continuum depend on others for their feelings of self-worth, and if they encounter conflict or failure they may have a hard time bouncing back from it. If they take on an initiative in their job and it fails, they may not volunteer for another one. Insecure people who experience a failure may spend their entire career in the safety of their cubicle, unwilling to put themselves out there a second time around. These people don't understand something that all narcissists know: Failure is not fatal and success is not permanent.

Most of us experience setbacks and feel self-doubt from time to time, and although we may lie low for a while, we usually recover in a reasonable amount of time. We say to ourselves, "Well, *that* project didn't work out so well. I guess I'll have to try a different strategy next time!" But those at the low end of the continuum tend to think of every failure, even relatively minor ones, as a major catastrophe. They deride themselves. "That project bombed because I'm bad," they think. "I'm a terrible person. I have never been good at anything. I never will be good at anything. I should just give up because I'm worthless. I don't deserve success." For these people, every failure tends to feed into a cycle of self-hatred.

Kenny is a good example of this kind of personality. Here is how he described himself when he wrote to me on my website: "I tend to underestimate myself in almost everything I do. For example, when I play a sport I think, how am I able to do this? When I sit in lectures I speculate, how do I think I am able to understand what is being said? I am in dire need of help."

Kenny clearly struggled with *severe* insecurity, and was probably a zero or one on the continuum. I advised him to identify a few things he was good at and to find ways to build on those small positives. Little successes can add up and help build self-confidence. Success breeds confidence, while failure just breeds doubt.

I probably don't need to say that this kind of self-doubt is not an issue for narcissistic people. These folks—the ones who are a six or seven or higher on the continuum—have an amazing ability to maintain their self-confidence in the face of failure. If a self-focused individual fails at a project, he can bounce back and move on to the next one without thinking twice. Sometimes this resilience strikes outsiders as naïve or a little bit crazy. "Doesn't he realize that plan is *never* going to work?" But self-focused individuals have great faith that they will succeed. And of course, persistence is often the key to success.

Because self-focused folks have such a strong sense of self, they rarely get caught up in an identity crisis or suffer from existential doubt. Even when others see evidence to the contrary, self-focused people think of themselves as good, valuable, and strong. They genuinely believe that they deserve to be successful in life.

Of course, for people who are higher on the continuum, that belief gets exaggerated. Those who are eights and above may go beyond thinking of themselves as decent people who deserve a good life. They view themselves as great, wildly talented, and deserving of fame and fortune. To envision this kind of self-focus, look no further than Charlie Sheen, who described himself as someone with tiger blood and Adonis DNA. "I'm tired of pretending like I'm not special, I'm tired of pretending like I'm not bitching, a total fricking rock star from Mars."[1] In certain kinds of environments, where there is a high rate of failure and little social support, that kind of self-confidence is essential to success. That's why so many famous actors, politicians, and CEOs are high on the self-focus continuum. Without a high self-regard they would be unable to muster the courage necessary to go up against intense competition and seek extremely challenging roles and positions. That self-regard also has its downsides. It can make the CEO or politician seem unapproachable to others. It can give them a sense of entitlement that leads them to take liberties that most of us would consider inappropriate. And because they have such a heightened sense of respect for themselves, they sometimes display a pronounced *lack* of respect for anyone whom they consider to be weak or insecure. Aides, advisers, employees, spouses, and children beware!

Toward the ten end of the continuum lies what I call pathological narcissism, or narcissistic personality disorder. While we hope that most CEOs and politicians consider themselves to be public servants, at least to *some* degree, true narcissists care only about themselves and think little, if at all, about others. They don't take into account the pain and suffering they might cause others and, if they do notice it, they don't see it as significant. These people will lie, cheat, steal, backstab—and they do it without a sense of responsibility, because it's all part of getting what they want and think they so richly deserve. For these folks, it's all about maximizing their personal wealth, fame, success, and desires at the expense of everyone else.

But these people are still basically functioning members of society, though they may leave emotional havoc in their wake. At the very, very furthest reaches of the continuum—think ten-plus-plus-plus—are the people who have a narcissistic personality coupled with a criminal mind. These are society's sociopaths, and they can bring devastation to anyone who knows them and to the communities they live in.

It's a tough crowd at the far end of the narcissism continuum.

REDEFINING NARCISSISTIC PERSONALITY DISORDER

These days, if we call someone a narcissist, we're being judgmental and usually speaking with a negative spin. When Dietrich's family accused him of being a narcissist, they weren't saying that he was wonderfully self-confident, ambitious, and charismatic. No, they meant that he was self-absorbed and completely out of touch with the feelings of his family and friends.

We can date the derogatory definition of narcissism back thousands of years. According to the ancient Greek myth, Narcissus was an extraordinarily beautiful young man. Maidens and nymphs were constantly falling in love with him, but he refused all of their advances. Finally, one of the nymphs was so smitten by Narcissus and in such despair when he rejected her that she sent up a prayer to the gods, pleading that he be punished for his selfishness. A goddess heard the nymph's prayer, took pity on her, and placed a curse on the gorgeous young man. If Narcissus wanted to reject the love of all those around him, he would be doomed to fall in love with himself. One day, Narcissus caught sight of his own image, reflected in the waters of a fountain. He did exactly as the goddess had decreed. He became utterly enamored of his own good looks and gazed at himself until he faded away into death. Even as his spirit crossed the river into Hades, he could not take his eyes away from his reflection.

Our current understanding of pathological narcissism (narcissistic personality disorder, or NPD) evolved from this ancient example. In the DSM-IV, NPD is defined as "a pervasive pattern of grandiosity (in fantasy or behavior), need for admiration, and lack of empathy." To be diagnosed with NPD, an individual must exhibit certain symptomatic traits including a "grandiose sense of self-importance," a preoccupation with "fantasies of unlimited success" (both terms come from the DSM), the belief that they are special or unique, the tendency to exploit others, and the need for excessive admiration.

I should note here that NPD will reportedly be eliminated from the DSM-V. I hope this will be a positive step toward a different understanding of the narcissistic continuum. But who could argue that the Bernie Madoffs, Rod Blagojeviches, or Charlie Sheens of the world are not pathological narcissists in need of treatment?

There are three important things to understand about narcissistic personality disorder. The first is that pathological narcissists are totally out of touch with reality. We expect that self-focused and successful individuals should receive respect and recognition for their achievements—*after* they have achieved them. We laud the politician who wins a tough election, reward the brilliant scientist with a Nobel Prize nomination, and recognize a talented author with excellent reviews and healthy sales. Pathological narcissists, however, want and expect to be recognized for their greatness even before they've achieved anything at all.

A second important point about narcissism is that when it's pathological, it often covers up a deep sense of inadequacy. We call this "overcompensating." People who actually feel bad about themselves will often build a grandiose fortress of greatness in their own minds and try to convince others that it is real. Bullying is a small-scale example of this kind of behavior. Children often bully because they aren't confident in themselves. Similarly, adults will pursue the superficial markings of strength and success. They may buy mansions and jets, name drop, grasp at any opportunity for self-promotion, and generally do whatever they can to put themselves forward and make others feel beneath them.

The final important point I want to make is that people with NPD can be extremely abusive. Self-focused individuals all along the continuum can be difficult to get along with, because their ambition and self-confidence may be intimidating or off-putting. A good example of this is William. As a lawyer and the CEO of a successful company in a very competitive industry, William has extremely high expectations of his employees. He pushes people hard, and for the more sensitive among them, his hard-driving nature can sometimes be frustrating—especially since William often expects others to exhibit behaviors (organizational skills, for example) that he doesn't exhibit himself.

But William is not a pathological narcissist. His high expectations, although occasionally frustrating, largely work to inspire his employees rather than intimidate them or crush their spirits.

People with NPD, on the other hand, tend to be abusive or manipulative of others and absorbed with themselves. Two astounding examples of this kind of behavior that have come to light recently are Rod Blagojevich and Bernie Madoff. Both men behaved as if the rules that govern society did not apply to them—as if they were above societal norms. Blagojevich reportedly tried to engage in illegal activities on a phone that he knew was tapped, flaunting his behavior in the face of the public.

Madoff's behavior, of course, was much, much worse. His Ponzi scheme resulted in the loss of billions of dollars, affected thousands of people all over the world, and was particularly destructive to the charitable foundations that trusted him with the funds that were their lifeblood. So Madoff's behavior not only hurt wealthy people who presumably had some understanding of the risks inherent in investing on such a big scale. It also had significant implications for many of his clients who were not particularly savvy investors and who relied on the returns from Madoff's firm to conduct their philanthropic work around the world.

The truly astounding aspect of Madoff's behavior is that it was inevitable that he would get caught. As one journalist pointed out, schemes of this kind have been around a long time (even before Charles Ponzi, who ran a notorious such scheme in the 1920s, came along) and almost always end in failure and ruin. Eventually, the fraudster is unable to attract enough new money to keep paying out a return to the earlier investors. One day it all collapses and the fraud is exposed. Only a person who truly believes that the rules do not apply to him—that, despite the internal logic of the scheme, he will never get caught—would attempt a Ponzi scheme to begin with.[2]

That kind of behavior is characteristic of a pathological narcissist. Madoff flaunted his "success" by creating an ostentatious lifestyle with his stolen money. He owned jets, a yacht, a Manhattan penthouse, and much more. His apparent wealth fueled people's admiration for him and encouraged them to invest still more with his company. When it all came crashing down, Madoff showed no concern for the victims of his scheme. Even before the disaster struck, he is reported to have been cold and distant with people he interacted with in his business and personal life.[3]

Madoff is the most egregious example of this kind of narcissistic behavior but hardly the only one. We have seen that our society often rewards a similar kind of narcissism. Many of those people whose actions helped trigger the 2008 financial crisis and subsequent recession exhibit narcissistic traits. As of this writing, most of those people are still wealthy, still employed, and still focused on personal gain after we the taxpayers bailed them out.

Clearly, pathological narcissism is a troubling disorder that, as in the case of Bernard Madoff, can have consequences not just for those who suffer from it but for all the rest of us. That's why it's so important that folks learn to understand narcissism as a continuum trait. As a society, we need to recognize the link between healthy narcissism (self-confidence and ambition) and pathological narcissism (overinflated egos and abusive behavior). That way we can celebrate and reward the positive behaviors, while condemning the destructive kind.

An Evolutionary Imperative

Modern psychiatry has defined narcissism in a rather rigid way, as a mental disorder that fits specific criteria. But in fact, narcissism is one of the most basic personality types that can be traced back not just to the Stone Age village, but to our earliest and most animal instincts.

It turns out it's not just humans who can be narcissists. Scientists have found that alpha males in primate groups meet all of the diagnostic criteria for narcissistic personality disorder in the DSM-IV. This is particularly true of chimpanzees. When seeking alpha male status, chimpanzees exhibit envy of their leaders, make strategic alliances to gain power, and seek success, power, and control. After achieving power, these animals demand excessive admiration from subordinates and females, display a sense of entitlement to the best food and dwelling places, are arrogant toward lower-ranking individuals, are exploitative of their inferiors and harass them.[4]

We would likely view these as negative traits if we were to encounter them in males in today's society. Yet as one researcher points out, "In an evolutionary sense alpha males are successful individuals."[5] He argues that in the context of primate societies, alpha males are exhibiting nothing more sinister than a "healthy narcissism."

This healthy narcissism is what we see in action in the Stone Age village. In prehistoric times, the healthy narcissist, or self-focused individual, would have been the alpha male of the tribe. (Scientists point out that among a certain type of chimpanzee, the bonobo, females are dominant, but the role is essentially the same.) He or, less commonly, she would have been the leader of the tribe in times of struggle or warfare. He would have been confident in his decision making, convincing and even inspiring in his leadership style, careful to manage his relationships among the powerful members of the group, and courageous in times of war. Furthermore, just as chimpanzee groups occasionally have "good and wise" alpha males, the self-focused human leader of a Stone Age village might not have been abusive. If he was a little lower on the self-focused continuum, he might have been empathic and considerate in his leadership role—the "benevolent dictator" of the Stone Age village.

In prehistoric times, self-focused individuals were necessary for the survival of the tribe. Sigmund Freud, the father of modern psychiatry, must have recognized the evolutionary imperative of narcissism. He identified it as one of only three major personality types. The first type he identified was the *erotic* type. Folks with erotic personalities tend to be emotional and loving. (This is a different use of the word "erotic" than in "erotic literature" and doesn't have a whole lot to do with sex.) Dramatic and adventurous personalities probably fall into this category.

Freud's second personality type was *obsessive*. Obsessive personalities are self-directed, organized, and efficient. Perfectionist and anxious personalities fall into this category.

Freud's third category is the narcissistic personality. The important thing to remember here is that Freud wasn't *pathologizing* narcissism when he used it as a label; he wasn't suggesting that these people were ill or in need of treatment. (Although he worked with people whose narcissistic tendencies were so severe that they were unhealthy.) Instead, Freud saw it as one of the normal tendencies of human personality.[6] I'd speculate that if pushed, Freud would have been open to the idea of a continuum of narcissistic personality.

Ascendant Strengths

From primates to prehistoric villages to modern psychiatric thought, self-focused personalities can play an important role in society when they learn to tap in to their most positive characteristics. They are the leaders of groups, both animal and human. And they help us survive in times of struggle and strife.

If you are self-focused, you may exhibit the follow ascendant strengths:

ABILITY TO PERSUADE OTHERS You are a strong leader. You are motivated and have the ability to motivate others.

INNER STRENGTH You have a sense of destiny, a conviction about your mission in life. You are strongly motivated to make your mark on the world.

RESILIENCE You have a certain level of confidence in the face of adversity or failure. You are usually well prepared for whatever difficulties the rest of your life brings. After a failure, you may feel unhappy, but never worthless. You can take life's setbacks in stride, though you may be put off balance for a time. Your resilience helps you survive a wide variety of criticism and competitive envy.

SELF-ESTEEM You feel good about yourself without needing constant reassurance about your worth. You often feel "special" or especially talented to a degree. Your self-esteem tends to be steady in the face of rejection, disapproval, or attacks. This can propel you to overcome mighty obstacles in your path.

HEALTHY BODY IMAGE You generally value your body and appearance, and therefore are more apt to take good care of your health. A study conducted by the National Weight Control Registry, a group that tracks people who have shed weight and kept it off long-term, found that a healthy narcissism was a key factor in long-term weight control. Most likely, you have a realistic body image too, created from within rather than from without. You can accept your body as imperfect, but still see it as worthy of being loved and cared for.

VISIONARY, STRATEGIC LEADERSHIP You are often the driving force of an enterprise or workplace. You are an innovator. You push harder than others. You have the skills to manage people well and lead new initiatives.

CALM UNDER PRESSURE Drawing on your unshakable self-belief, you perform brilliantly under pressure when others would crack. You can be invaluable in a crisis.

Current research suggests that people who are narcissistic tend to be less anxious, depressed, or lonely than others and often psychologically healthier. I'll discuss this more in a bit.

Living a Self-Focused Life

Self-focus can be a good thing. If you're a six or seven on the continuum, you exhibit ascendant strengths that make you well suited to success, especially in today's self-promotional environment. On the other hand, you may find it more difficult to manage a healthy relationship, which requires a partnership of equals—something that runs counter to the self-focused lifestyle. But by tapping in to your ascendant strengths and better understanding the contours of your personality profile, there's no reason why a self-focused lifestyle can't be a happy and healthy one.

Self-Focus in the Internet Age

Do you follow yourself closely on Twitter? Have you been blogging regularly about your coming memoir?

Do you make a habit of weeping about your values in public—or in front of videographers documenting your work?[7]

—New York Times, *December 4, 2010*

We live in a narcissistic age. The popular media spend a great deal of time bemoaning a new generation that is more self-promotional, self-absorbed, and entitled than ever before. The above *New York Times* article is just one example of this tendency. Social networking sites seem to make this trend abundantly clear.

Is there any truth to these concerns, or are these just the predictable fears that every generation has for the youth of today? I am skeptical of the idea that every generation is wildly different from the next. I think we all have a lot more in common than we usually realize. I tend to see any social change as evolutionary, and I think that entire societies change very slowly.

On the other hand, I do think there is some truth to the contention that the Internet has had a profound impact on today's youth. Current research backs me up. A recent study by Sara Konrath at the University of Michigan found that college students today are 40 percent less empathic than those thirty years ago. The empathy levels dropped most rapidly after the year 2000. Empathy, of course, is being able to feel and identify with the pain, problems, or predicaments of another, which prompts us to want to help. In today's *look at me, me, me* and *I want what I want when I want it and screw you if you get in my way* society, is it any wonder that empathy has declined?

Dr. Konrath admitted that "we don't actually know what the

causes are at this point." But it's thought that video games, social media, texting, reality TV, and hypercompetition—all part of growing up in the twenty-first century—have something to do with it. My take: It's hard to feel empathy toward another when your contact is mainly through IM, texting, email, Facebook, and Twitter. The people seem less real.

This is bad news for America's future. If we have less empathy it means that our relationships with one another will be less loving and caring. A relative lack of empathy might also be contributing to the rise in a host of troubling behaviors such as violence, aggression, and sexual offenses.[8]

Another small-scale study (which gathered data from just a hundred students) found that people who already have narcissistic tendencies often use social networking in a particular way. These people are more self-promotional than their peers. While others use the sites to chat with friends, keep in touch with distant relations, or share photos, these college students view Facebook, Myspace, and Twitter as channels that enable them to talk about themselves. They have a higher proportion of self-portraits than their peers. They are more likely to write about themselves, their achievements, and their goals.[9]

What this means is that today's social networking sites benefit people who were already narcissistic, just like reality TV shows that put people on screen to celebrate themselves and prove their worth. In other words, these sites are part of a rising societal tendency to encourage and even celebrate narcissism. Someone who's a seven on the continuum might be more likely to play up that side of her personality when she has access to Facebook than she would have been twenty years ago.

If a YouTube video of your performance with a church choir has the potential to make you a star (as it did for Justin Bieber), posting the video is not just narcissistic; it could be a savvy and rational career move.

That's why it's so important for self-focused individuals to think seriously about their personality profile. As I said before, there has never been a better time to be self-focused. The world loves and rewards those of us who exhibit the ascendant traits of the self-focused personality.

But that doesn't excuse abusive behaviors. Bullying, violence, and other negative aspects of narcissism are consequences of a self-aggrandizing society that we cannot accept. Self-focused individuals have a responsibility to learn to live in an empathic way regardless of their personality type. Then you can go ahead and take advantage of the great opportunities that the new millennium offers to people like you.

A Narcissist at Work

In his book *The Productive Narcissist,* Michael Maccoby describes a new kind of CEO that began to appear in the 1990s. These leaders are high profile. Their faces appear on magazines, and they speak publicly about everything from business leadership to lifestyle, family, philosophy, and politics. They are celebrity CEOs, working not just for financial success but for fame and influence. Larry Ellison (CEO of Oracle), Jack Welch (GE), and George Soros are examples of leaders who are included in this category.

Maccoby argues that these leaders, though not pathological, exhibit narcissistic personalities. But he calls them "productive narcissists"—that is, they bring the best qualities of a narcissistic personality into the forefront in order to lead their businesses to great success.

The successful, self-focused business leader is certainly a category that I have observed in my years as a clinical psychiatrist. And it's one that business leaders themselves tend to be aware of. As Dietrich put it, "Anybody who wants to be a CEO is probably narcissistic, because you have to constantly want everybody to look at you and want to be at the top of the pyramid and to be the one to do the things that everybody else says is great."

You may remember Dietrich from the "Adventurous" chapter (chapter 2), where he talked about his need for action in the workplace, and how it compelled him to leave his accounting career for a more adventurous lifestyle.

But it wasn't just Dietrich's adventurous personality that led him to a new career. Dietrich was ambitious—he wanted, as he said, to be the center of attention, to be successful. He believed that he was destined for greatness.

At first, Dietrich thought he would become a writer, so he attained an internship in computer support for a national publication and wrote what he calls a "frightening type of fiction" on the side. But, he said, "I was never really any good. It was hard, and it just wasn't natural." Fiction clearly wasn't the right path for Dietrich, so he focused on business writing instead for a while, until he decided to pursue entrepreneurship.

Becoming an entrepreneur was a smart career move for Dietrich. He loved the adventure of starting a new business and his self-focused personality gave him the self-confidence to keep going when no one else believed in him. Even though his move was risky, I commend Dietrich for following the path that best fit his personality traits and ascendant strengths—and for having faith that the rest would fall into place.

The best part about Dietrich's career shift is that even though the job has changed significantly since his entrepreneurial days, Dietrich still gets to use his greatest strengths on the job. As the CEO of a successful business, he is able to bring his self-focus to bear on his corporate leadership. Dietrich has found a place for himself as a productive narcissist.

My colleague Leonard is a little closer to the middle of the self-focus continuum. At about a six, Leonard doesn't need the leadership role and attention that Dietrich gets every day. (Actually, anxiety is more dominant in Leonard's personality profile; he also appeared in chapter 5.)

But in his professional life, Leonard works hard to *represent* people, many of whom he deems to be narcissists. He helps manage their affairs and is part of the complex system that allows these people to achieve success.

"I don't need to be in the spotlight myself," Leonard said, "because my clients are." Leonard has achieved a good balance between his anxiety and his self-focus. He likes representing important people, but he works best behind the scenes, where he can keep his anxiety under control. Leonard's life provides a good example of the ways in which you can take advantage of your self-focused trait without needing to be number one. And his ability to balance several dominant personality traits is commendable.

Other careers in which self-focused individuals excel include politics and performance—professions where you can stand alone, earn attention and respect from those around you, and lead the pack. Even if you aren't in one of these careers, you can put your latent self-focus to work by leading a departmental project, chairing a committee, or founding an organization, club, or team outside of work. If your life path hasn't set you up to be in the spotlight, that doesn't mean you can't take advantage of your ascendant strengths.

Self-Focused Relationships

Narcissists often have particular difficulty navigating and managing personal relationships. They tend to go through a string of connections that don't last long and are usually lacking in intimacy. The narcissistic personality can cause problems in a marriage or long-term relationship.

When I first met my friend Andrew, for example, I was immediately impressed by his remarkable charisma and commanding presence. I wasn't surprised to learn that he had enjoyed a highly successful career in politics. However, at the time, Andrew was hardly feeling on top of the world. He'd just lost his bid to be elected to Congress and was estranged from his wife of many years. Andrew confided in me that his political career and his marriage were over and he had to "rediscover himself."

To Andrew's credit, he was willing to take a hard look at himself. When he did, he was able to recognize that he'd always put his own needs before those of his family and his political colleagues. He began to see that his excessive focus on himself had blinded him to the emotional and psychological needs of others around him. He found this self-examination "eye-opening" and dedicated himself to change.

Today Andrew is happier than he's ever been. He has remarried and found a second career as a highly successful consultant. He's channeled his strengths—his charisma and his leadership qualities—into his new life while maintaining a markedly increased level of self-awareness born of his period of failure and self-reflection. He is more empathic to others, spends time with his three young kids, and is able to meaningfully say that he's a great husband and father. And his new wife agrees with that assessment.

When we had talked about his strengths, Andrew felt that in addition to his leadership and social skills, he was resilient—definitely an ascendant strength of a narcissist. Resilient individuals tend to have more satisfying relationships, because they can withstand those inevitable crises that can disable a family—like a serious illness, a death, work failures, depression, or prolonged bouts of stress or anxiety. Andrew realized he had the strength to remain steady and strong and keep the family safe—a realization that played well to the positive aspects of his narcissism. By being more empathic, expressing his feelings, and using his resilience, Andrew moved to a point on the continuum where his narcissistic tendencies had a positive effect on the relationship.

Andrew's experience proves that it can be challenging to be in a relationship with a self-focused individual. You might fall in love with her for her charisma, leadership, and professional success. But when it comes to the hard work of making a relationship stick, self-focused individuals can be frustrating to live with. They tend to put their own ambitions before their spouse and children. You might feel neglected romantically, or as though your own achievements and goals don't matter.

The first important thing is to ask yourself whether your spouse is giving you the respect you deserve. While many "yin-and-yang" relationships work well, in this case a strong self-focused personality, when paired with a quieter personality, can make it even more difficult for the quiet person to assert himself (or herself). In some cases (if one partner is too far up the narcissistic scale, and if the quieter person is low in self-confidence), it can even lead to emotional abuse. That's what happened to my friend Linda. She married a successful neurosurgeon, and for a while they were deeply in love. But slowly, her husband began to take out his own insecurities on her. (Remember, self-focus can often be a cover for deep-seated self-doubt.) Linda's husband was constantly putting her down, calling her stupid, and accusing her children (from a previous marriage) of being lazy, ugly, and useless.

If you are in this kind of relationship, the best thing you can do for yourself is to get out. You cannot expect a ten-plus narcissist to change for you. Linda and her husband have gone to couples therapy several times, but her husband was never really committed to the process and as soon as each session ended, he returned to his habits. One hopes that he and others like him will find a way to make change stick. But if you are in an emotionally (or physically) abusive relationship, you owe it to yourself to exit now. Remember that you can't change who a person is: He is who he is.

On the other hand, if your spouse is a healthy, self-focused individual, there are things you can do to help your relationship work.

The first thing is to try to understand what the self-focused personality type is, and what its ascendant strengths are. I hope this chapter has helped you with that.

Does your partner live a lifestyle that maximizes the ascendant strengths while minimizing the accompanying weaknesses? If not, think of ways to help your spouse channel his or her personality. When our self-focused spouses are satisfied professionally, they are less likely to feel insecure or frustrated at home. And if their self-focus becomes self-absorption, speak up! Sometimes it just takes a little prod from outside to help a self-focused person get back on track.

Self-focused people can have healthy and satisfying relationships when both partners are honest with each other. People whose dominant trait is narcissism do well with people who can complement or balance their personality and keep them in check. Shy individuals can help a self-focused individual stay grounded. Magical thinkers can bring a different perspective to someone who often has a one-track mind. And people who fall on the OCD continuum partner well with narcissists, because they can bring an attention to detail that narcissists often lack. In return, narcissists provide focus, energy, and a bigger-picture view of the world, resulting in a symmetrical, and satisfying, relationship.

Conclusion: Are You Self-Focused?

Where do you fall on the narcissistic continuum? People who are high in this trait have a tendency to underestimate where they fall on the scale, so I strongly recommend you take the time to fill out the questionnaire in the appendix. You may be surprised by what you find.

If you filled out the questionnaire and found yourself to be high on this trait, you may be feeling a little bit defensive right now.

"I'm not a narcissist!" you might think. "I care about other people. I'm not concerned solely with myself."

If you read this chapter, you understand that pathological narcissism differs from someone who's a seven or so on the narcissistic continuum, for example, in several key ways. Self-focused folks are usually ambitious, driven, confident, and charismatic, while people with the superdominant trait may be abusive toward others, delusional about their own strengths, and irrational in their choices.

But it's worth taking a good hard look at whether you show any of the negative tendencies associated with narcissism. Do your loved ones berate you for not remembering their birthdays or making sure they get the attention they deserve? Do you feel a sense of entitlement, expecting others to change their schedules or rearrange their lives to suit your needs? Do you sometimes get uncontrollably angry when you feel you've been wronged?

If so, it's important that you take the time to think about whether these actions are standing in the way of your relationships or your happiness. You may think that you need to behave this way in order to achieve success. Is that really the case? Is it worth it?

And what about the ascendant strengths of narcissism? What role do those strengths play in your life? If narcissism is your dominant trait, then you are probably already aware of your ascendant strengths: self-confidence, charisma, and resilience, among others. Don't force yourself to suppress these strengths. Instead, embrace your narcissism to tap in to the undiscovered strengths of your personality. Just don't get carried away with yourself.

EIGHT high energy BIPOLAR

In 2009, I started dividing my time between New York City and Lake Charles, Louisiana. The move to New York was part of a bigger move—reducing the time I spent operating the clinic and spending more time working toward my goal of helping people across America understand my core message: *You are who you are and you are better than normal.*

At first, I thought I'd start out simple. I built my website as an early way to spread my message while I developed this book. But I never expected to get a call from HLN—they had seen videos on the site and invited me to appear on the show *Issues with Jane Velez-Mitchell* in February 2009.

When I look back on that time now, it's hard for me to remember how I managed it all. I'd spend three or four days a week in Lake Charles, where I continued my psychiatric practice. Then I'd devote three days to running around New York, dashing from studio to studio, responding to requests for interviews and spreading my message wherever I could. I also had other professional commitments in Colorado, working on a talk show, and in Texas, where I was the corporate medical director for a twenty-facility drug treatment organization. And then there was my family. I was divorced but my daughter was living in New York and my son was, well, traveling somewhere in China. My sister and my parents were (and still are) in Louisiana.

That kind of schedule would be considered an exhausting one for most, but I didn't think of it that way. I felt as if I was running on some extra source of energy that kept me going for weeks at a time. In retrospect, I might call my state of mind at that time "hypomanic." Technically, a hypomanic episode is a period of increased energy that is less severe than full-blown mania. When you're hypomanic you are totally wired and full of creative energy. You tend to be more impulsive. You sleep less than usual. Your brain works faster than it used to and you often make connections that you couldn't have made before.

Hypomania can also include greater risk-taking and pleasure-seeking behavior, but I remember those days as being a lot of work, and virtually no—as in *no*—play.

I couldn't have done what I was doing that first year in New York if I hadn't tapped in to my hypomanic energy. Every once in a while, however, I would find myself with an unbooked weekend. My rational mind, the side of me that was still going at a hundred miles an hour, said: *Great! A free weekend!*

My body felt differently. My last appearance of the week would often be aired on Friday, and we'd be done at about four o'clock. I would walk from the CNN offices to my apartment. On the way, I'd swing by Whole Foods and pick up enough groceries to last me a couple of days. By five o'clock, I'd be in my apartment. I wouldn't step out the door again until Monday morning.

At first, I found those weekends a little depressing. I'd think about the list of things I should have been doing—the friends I really did want to call, the show I fully intended to see. I've always been a pretty active guy, and I usually follow the mantra: You can sleep when you're dead. I wasn't used to sitting around.

But the mental exhaustion, and the lethargy that came with it, was out of my control. I needed that weekend time to recharge. So finally I told myself, *You know what? You see people every day. You're working with people every day. And you have a goal that you are focused on, something bigger than yourself.* I reasoned that once I got the new career up and running, I would have free time once again, but right now, nothing was more important than what I was doing.

I also was aware that sleep is probably the single most important thing we can do to keep ourselves healthy. Once I accepted that, it became easy to embrace that idea that my weekends off were a way to recharge the batteries so that I could start my crazy life again at 6 A.M. Monday morning.

Now I'm able to maintain a more reasonable schedule. Interestingly, now that I no longer need to expend so much energy, I find that I don't have as much as I used to. I get tired more quickly than I did during that crazy period, but I also am able to leave my house on the weekends and get a good dinner or go out with friends. The year of extreme highs and extreme lows is over, at least for now. I have to admit, though, that at times I do miss it.

Even with less energy, I think of myself as having a high-energy profile. I fluctuate between long stretches of mildly hypomanic behavior and short periods when my energy levels are depressed. I'd say that I'm about an eight on the bipolar continuum.

Now, understand that my way was not the only way to do what I did. Some folks who are low on the bipolar trait are good at pacing themselves through such an extreme, time-intensive situation. They would perhaps do a bit less each day, but not need the weekend crashes as I did. And that's fine. It's all about knowing yourself and your traits and putting them to maximum use. For me, high-intensity energy was the way to go.

At the far reaches of the high-energy continuum is bipolar disorder. I want to clarify up front that of course, bipolar disorder—

which is characterized by full-blown *manic* episodes, often with matching *major depressive* episodes—is a devastating mental disorder. Living with bipolar disorder is a struggle that I will discuss later in this chapter.

But if your energy levels fluctuate the way mine do—between long periods of high energy that are hugely productive, and short periods of exhaustion and recharging—then you are a privileged individual. With awareness and a thoughtfully structured life, you can follow this trait down exciting and positive pathways, just as I have.

THE CONTINUUM MODEL: HIGH ENERGY

BIPOLAR CONTINUUM				
FLAT MOOD		INSPIRED MOOD		BIPOLAR
0	3	5	7	10+
Absent		Dominant		Superdominant

A popular exercise among psychiatrists (and their patients) is to make a mood graph. To do so, take a sheet of graph paper and draw a horizontal line across the middle to represent a neutral mood. (I'll be honest—I have a hard time remembering what a "neutral mood" actually feels like.) Then, on the left-hand vertical edge, or Y axis, mark the numbers one through ten above the line, and the numbers minus one through minus ten below the line. On the bottom horizontal edge, or X axis, mark the day. (See the chart below.) Each day, make a mark on the paper that approximates your mood. If you're feeling good, rank your mood in the positive numbers. If you're feeling down, rate your mood in the negative numbers.

The range of moods, of course, is infinite. But over time, you may begin to see certain patterns. You might discover that although you feel as if your mood swings a lot, it actually remains within a relatively narrow range. If that's the case, you're probably toward the zero end of the bipolar continuum. People who fall on this part of the spectrum are often reliable, stable, and cautious. You're not easily shaken by dramatic events. You're probably persistent and rational in your behavior. "Steady as she goes" would define your personality.

On the other hand, you may find that your mood fluctuates a lot more than that. Some people are high most of the time, with occasional drops (that's how I am). Some people seem to go up and down on a day-to-day basis (you'll see that a lot in those with dramatic personalities).

People with bipolar personalities can vary in the frequency and severity of their energy swings. This graphic compares a person who would be about a three on the continuum with someone who's about a seven:

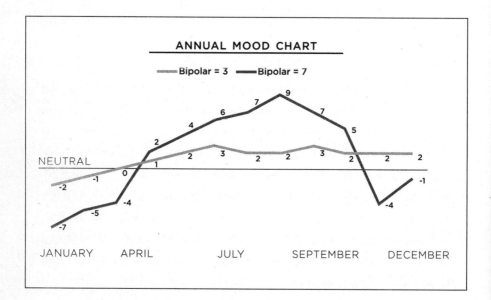

If you have a high-energy personality, you might want to try keeping a mood chart like this one over a long period of time. As you do so, look for patterns in the times when you feel high and when you feel low. Are they caused by certain things, such as a new job or a major disappointment? Or do they seem to cycle on a monthly or annual basis? As you'll see later in this chapter, learning to predict and manage the shifts in your moods is a key to living a high-energy life that is also stable.

REDEFINING BIPOLAR DISORDER

At the far end of the bipolar continuum, you may start experiencing symptoms that fall into the category of bipolar disorder. In order to better discuss my preferred way of looking at this disorder, I would like to introduce a young man named Marc Peters. Marc is a special figure in this book. While all of the stories in this book are true, I have changed the names and some of the identifying characteristics of most folks in order to respect their privacy.

Marc requested that I use his real name. As an active advocate for those with mental disorders, Marc puts himself and his story in the public eye every day to live his message and destigmatize mental illness. Marc is a model of what it means to live and be successful with a diagnosis of bipolar disorder. That's why he was invited to be a part of this book.

When Marc was a freshman in college, it looked as if everything was going his way. Despite a teenage diagnosis of major depressive disorder, Marc had been "phenomenally successful" in high school, and he says that in the most humble way possible. He had written for major newspapers. He had won national scholarships. "I was heading off to college like a real success," he told me. "I had a ridiculous trajectory.

"And, obviously, I crashed and burned."

In the first semester, things seemed to be going great. Marc was really enthusiastic about college life. He joined every club—and I mean *every* club—that he could find. He overloaded on coursework. He got into playing online poker.

In retrospect, he says, it's obvious that he was entering that hypomanic stage, which I described earlier. In his case it was the precursor to a full-blown manic episode. "I found myself asking a lot of my friends to read stuff I had written for class. All the work was fine, but I couldn't sit down long enough to edit it. I couldn't get myself under control enough to sit still."

In the DSM-IV, hypomania is defined as "a distinct period of persistently elevated, expansive, or irritable mood, lasting at least four days." To be hypomanic, a person's mood and behavior during that time must be *unequivocally* different from his or her normal state. Hypomanic individuals tend to be more talkative than usual. They show an increase in goal-directed activity. They tend to experience a flight of ideas. ("It can be hard for people to keep up with my line of thought because it's speeding along so fast," Marc says.) They show a decreased need for sleep. They are easily distracted.

One thing that I find remarkable about the symptoms of hypomania is how appealing they sound. Don't we all want to be someone who doesn't need sleep, is really active and involved, talkative, quick thinking, and goal oriented?

I believe that there are some who live most of their lives in a hypomanic state. I'm close to being one of them! They never see a doctor about their condition, however, because it doesn't seem abnormal to them, and because it's not fundamentally detrimental.

Others experience hypomania in a way that has a serious negative impact on their lives. These folks are diagnosed with either cyclothymia or bipolar II disorder. Cyclothymia is characterized by mood swings between hypomanic episodes and mild depressive episodes. To receive a bipolar II diagnosis, a person must experience major depressive episodes. If the person experiences full-blown mania, he receives a diagnosis of bipolar I.

As you can probably tell, there are many, many different kinds of mood disorders, and they fall along a spectrum of severity. On the depressed side, there is dysthymic disorder (mild depression) and major depression. On the manic side, there is hypomania and mania. These mood episodes can influence people's lives in a variety of ways, and to varying degrees. They can also combine and mix and match. It all depends on the person and the symptoms.

This is why bipolar disorder is already thought of in the psychiatric community as a spectrum disorder. The next step is for psychiatry to realize that the spectrum extends beyond disorders and into healthy behavior as well—that the distinction between "normal" and "abnormal" is often a matter of perception. It's not about whether you have bipolar or you don't. Instead, it's about where you fall on the bipolar continuum. If you're far enough up the scale, you may need treatment.

Now, back to Marc. When we left him, he was enjoying a hyperactive, hypomanic first year of college. He was now in his second semester, and spring break was fast approaching. While some students consider spring break a chance to relax and have fun (especially students who are maintaining a grueling schedule, as Marc was), he decided to do something different. I'll let Marc tell the story.

"Rather than go home and rest on spring break, I decided to do a Habitat for Humanity service trip and went down to Florida. We were doing a blitz build on a house. Sometime during the drive from Syracuse to Florida, my mania pushed over into psychotic behavior. I was hearing the voice of God and being told to act a certain way. I stopped making any kind of rational decisions and completely broke from reality."

Marc was experiencing a transition from hypomania into a full-blown manic episode with psychotic symptoms on top. When did this transition occur? That's a tough question. When does productive hypomania cross the line into full-blown mania? To put it simply: When you can live your life the way you choose, then you probably are okay. Once you cannot—and by Marc's own admission he could no longer function rationally—that line is crossed.

But it's important to understand that sometimes the individual is the last person to realize that he has crossed that line, simply because he isn't thinking rationally. Often people who are undergoing a true manic episode don't make the connection until after treatment. That's when they look back and say, "Wow! I was really sick!"

Furthermore, Marc's case is remarkable because he experienced the most severe symptom of mania: psychosis. In the case of psychosis, it's safe to say that treatment is *always* needed. But it's important to realize that in most cases, a manic individual may lose his ability to function in the world without ever having a psychotic episode. He may still benefit from psychiatric help, by which I mean both medication and therapeutic support.

I wouldn't call my hypomanic periods "mania" even though they can last for weeks. On the other hand, psychosis was a clear sign that Marc needed treatment. Kay Redfield Jamison, one of the world's foremost experts on bipolar disorder, describes the transition well. In her memoir *An Unquiet Mind,* she writes about a manic episode that she experienced during her first year on the faculty at UCLA.

"I did not wake up one day to find myself mad. Life should be so simple. Rather, I gradually became aware that my life and mind were going at an ever faster and faster clip until finally, over the course of my first summer on the faculty, they both had spun wildly and absolutely out of control. But the acceleration from quick thought to chaos was a slow and beautifully seductive one."[1]

I'll talk more about the seduction of hypomania later, and about the importance of recognizing when and how to manage a hypomanic episode. As I said earlier, hypomania can be a highly productive and often pleasurable experience. Manic episodes, on the other hand, are severe. As Marc explained, "Up to a certain point it's harmless, and then it's dangerous."

When Marc heads into a manic episode (he's had more than one) all of his hypomanic tendencies get more severe. As an example, Marc spoke about generosity. "I'm a generous person anyway," he says. "I'll be generous with my time, I'll be generous with resources. I've had a lot of people help me get where I am, so anything I can do for friends, I'm very, very willing to do. I don't see generosity as a flaw until the point when I flip into mania and I'm starting to spend a lot more money and I'm making irrational purchases. I'm doing all these things that are detrimental and are unsafe."

Sexual risk taking, drug use, and violence increase during manic episodes, although Marc says he's lucky that he has never abused drugs or been violent.

Eventually, an individual undergoing a manic episode will cease to function altogether. When Virginia Woolf was manic, according to her husband, Leonard, "She talked almost without stopping for two or three days, paying no attention to anyone in the room or anything said to her. For about a day what she said was coherent; the sentences meant something, though it was nearly all wildly insane. Then gradually it became completely incoherent, a mere jumble of dissociated words."[2]

Robert Lowell, a poet famous for his bipolar moods, wrote, "Seven years ago I had an attack of pathological enthusiasm. The night before I was locked up I ran about the streets of Bloomington, Indiana, crying out against devils and homosexuals. I believed I could stop cars and paralyze their forces by merely standing in the middle of the highway with my arms outspread."[3]

In fact, hospitalization and arrest are common enough among

manic individuals that they are considered to be defining criteria of bipolar disorder.

I am dwelling on the severity of a true manic episode because I want to be clear about the meaning of bipolar disorder at its worst. Look no further than Charlie Sheen, who I suspect has this condition (of course I can't diagnose him without actually talking with him), or Mel Gibson, who admits to having been diagnosed bipolar in the past. This is not a disorder that I would wish on anyone, as much as I appreciate the positive aspects of the high-energy trait. No statistic provides more meaningful evidence to the struggles of bipolar disorder than the fact that the lifetime suicide risk for an individual suffering from bipolar disorder is 20 percent.[4] Furthermore, severe bipolar disorder is one of the most difficult psychiatric conditions to keep in check.

The good news is that in the last sixty years or so, psychiatry has made major breakthroughs in the treatment of bipolar disorder. In 1949, while studying the toxic effects of uric acid in guinea pigs, the Australian psychiatrist John Cade happened to notice that when the guinea pigs were injected with lithium carbonate, they became lethargic and unresponsive to stimuli without losing consciousness.

Cade realized that lithium might also be able to help psychotic patients, who often appear overstimulated. Early tests showed that his hypothesis was correct, and to this day lithium remains the medical community's treatment of choice for bipolar mood disorders.[5]

When lithium was first introduced for treatment of bipolar disorder, it was basically used as a human sedative. Bipolar patients were kept on a heavy dosage for years at a time, causing many patients to quit their medications. Kay Redfield Jamison, who began treatment for bipolar disorder years ago, writes that her medication made her so sedated that she could only read one paragraph of text at a sitting before she lost her ability to focus. That makes it all the more remarkable that she obtained her Ph.D. in psychology and became a tenured professor! If you're interested in an extraordinary story of recovery and perseverance through bipolar disorder, I recommend reading her memoir *An Unquiet Mind.*

Medication has come a long way. Today, lithium dosages are much lower than they once were, and they are prescribed in a carefully tailored fashion. Marc, for example, explained that after his first manic episode he was put on antipsychotics so strong he had a hard time focusing his eyes on anything—never mind his schoolbooks. It took more than a month of hospitalization before his doctors were able to find the combination and dosage of medications that were right for him.

Today, Marc lives most of his life without antipsychotics. Mood stabilizers and antidepressants help keep his mental state closer to neutral. He carefully monitors his moods on a day-by-day basis. And if he identifies any of the warning signals of an oncoming manic episode, he calls his psychiatrist and takes an antipsychotic, which he describes as a "reset button."

Marc also works closely with a therapist who provides cognitive and behavioral therapy to complement and reinforce the medications.

An Evolutionary Imperative

"When I got out of the hospital," Marc said in an interview, referring to his first manic episode, "I was completely shattered. I never thought that I would do anything of any kind of consequence ever again."

Marc had good reason to feel that way. The stigma around bipolar disorder is severe—the goal for most people is just to be well enough to lead a "normal" life. But of course, people with bipolar disorder—or anyone who has a high-energy personality—are hardly normal. High-energy folks live at the edges of human experience, and because of that, they have the potential not just to survive, but to do great things.

That's probably why natural selection has favored the survival of high-energy personalities—which have a strong genetic component—for millennia.

What is the genetic advantage of this sometimes devastating mental disorder? To begin to understand why this trait has survived for so long, let's return to our imaginary Stone Age village. Humans are living in small hunter-gatherer communities of 100 to 150 people. Some of these people (the narcissists) are the leaders of the pack. Some (the histrionics) are the entertainers and storytellers. The ADHD folks are the explorers.

But during times of battle or strife, the bipolar folks step up. These are people who experience huge bursts of courage during their hypomanic episodes. They are able to maintain their high energy for extensive periods of time without crashing or becoming exhausted. So when the Stone Age village is under attack from a competing group, or even during a high-risk battle with an animal that might eventually become dinner, these are the folks who take the lead.

The ability to fight and hunt well would have been enough to keep the hypomanic gene active for millennia. But week-long mammoth hunts are less common today than they were in the Stone Age. What's interesting is that the hypomanic trait has been adapted to benefit people living in a very, very different type of society—in modern civilization.

The first genetic benefit of bipolar disorder in the modern era is creativity. I know that I described hypomanic episodes as extremely creative, focused, and productive periods. Actually that description doesn't just come from me; it was written right into the DSM-IV definition of hypomania.

Heightened creativity and drive can be good in lots of ways. But one of the most positive things to come out of the hypomanic state throughout history has been art. Some of our greatest artists have been bipolar. Many of those who weren't, I imagine, still had a high-energy profile. A lot of people think of bipolar disorder as an artist's illness. As the scholar Robert Burton put it four hundred years ago, "All poets are mad."[6]

I'm talking about writers such as Edgar Allan Poe, Virginia Woolf, and Robert Lowell; painters such as Vincent van Gogh, Jackson Pollock, and Georgia O'Keeffe; musicians such as Pyotr Tchaikovsky, Irving Berlin, and Cole Porter.

Of course, bipolar disorder is a modern designation—just fifty years ago, the diagnosis was "manic-depressive," and a hundred years ago the diagnosis didn't exist. Classifying nonliving artists as bipolar requires a bit of speculation, but it is speculation based in scientific fact. All of these artists were carefully profiled by Jamison and found to meet stringent diagnostic criteria. If these artists weren't quite bipolar in the modern sense, they certainly had personalities and behavioral traits that match the diagnosis.

What's more, for at least the past four hundred years, artists have seen these bipolar tendencies as an important part of their artistic process. In the eighteenth century, in fact, Romantic poets in Britain described mania as a divinely inspired state, similar to the transcendence that classical Greek poets and seers were said to have achieved thousands of years before.[7] In fact, there is reason to think that yesterday's seers and prophets were not so different from today's bipolars and schizophrenics—more evidence that these diagnoses are evolving as we come to understand more about them.

What's interesting about the so-called myth of the crazy artist is that it has a basis in science. Jamison did a series of careful and comprehensive studies of historic and contemporary artists to determine whether they are more likely to be bipolar than the rest of us. She came back with a resounding yes!

The prevalence rate of bipolar disorder among artists is indeed higher than among the general public. And furthermore, most of the contemporary writers whom Jamison researched acknowledged that they had experienced states similar to what we call hypomanic—and that those states were essential to their writing process.

On the other hand, "mania"—the far end of the high-energy spectrum—isn't a positive or productive artistic state. Some, such as William James, credited the highs and lows of their moods with a unique ability to understand the full range of human experience. But while they may find this experience revelatory or transformational, most artists prefer to be a little bit closer to the middle of the continuum. Jamison found that artists who do suffer from bipolar disorder are actually more likely than their nonartistic peers to seek help if they find themselves losing control.

It's the high-energy state—*not* full-blown mania—that is so productive among the great artists and writers of our time.

So, although bipolar disorder is often associated with artists, another fascinating role that hypomania plays in society has been proposed in recent years. In his book *The Hypomanic Edge,* the clinical psychologist and author John Gartner proposes that hypomania, like ADHD, is also a trait common to explorers and adventurers—the type of people who pick up everything they have (or leave it all behind) and travel to an unknown or unfamiliar place in search of a new life. This is the second benefit that hypomania brings to modern society.

The implications are intriguing. Gartner suggests that immigrants, although we might not think of them as explorers, are genetically predisposed to be hypomanic. He says that for this reason, America is a country with a genetic predisposition to hypomania. And it is that hypomanic tendency that has fueled America's legacy of invention.

Here are some of the people Gartner includes in his list of hypo-manic or bipolar figures in American history:

Christopher Columbus, the explorer who set off across the seas and landed in America.

Alexander Hamilton, the most volatile and ambitious founding father.

Andrew Carnegie, America's great risk-taking industrialist and philanthropist.

The Selznick and Mayer families, the two great Hollywood founding families.

Craig Venter, the biologist and entrepreneur who first sequenced the human genome.

It is of course hard to state conclusively that Christopher Columbus, who died in 1506, was hypomanic, cyclothymic, or bipolar. But Gartner's methods of determining the mental state of these historic figures are interesting enough to describe here.

Gartner knew that we don't always have a whole lot of perspective on our own mental health. Are we energetic, high energy, hypomanic, or in need of mental health care? Are we tired, sad, depressed, or on the verge of a major depressive episode? Because it's so hard to know, doctors often refer to friends and family to find an outside perspective. There are well-established methods for interviewing people who are close to a patient in order to better evaluate the patient's mental health.

Gartner cleverly applied this technique to historical figures by interviewing the people closest to them—their biographers. He asked experts in the field to describe people such as Columbus or Hamilton based on diagnostic models. The results were positive. They may not have known it themselves, but Gartner believes these historical figures were surely hypomanic.

I think we can all learn from Gartner's technique. It's a good reminder that sometimes we don't have the perspective to know ourselves. I hope that this book, and the personality profile quizzes included, will help you better understand your own profile.

It's also helpful to realize that our loved ones may know us better than we know ourselves—that sometimes by asking them for help and wisdom we can gain a better perspective on ourselves.

And conversely, it's useful to remember that while we may see our friends and family clearly, they may not be nearly so self-aware. You might catch a loved one denying her true personality profile—trying to inhibit her anxiety, or clamp down on that adventurous spirit. Helping others understand themselves better in a compassionate way is another valuable tool that we can offer to our loved ones.

After examining the stories of some of America's heroes, Gartner came to the conclusion that hypomania is what gives America its entrepreneurial, creative, and inventive advantage.

Consider Christopher Columbus, for example. What "ordinary" person would approach the royalty of more than one country to seek funding for an ill-conceived and scientifically unfounded venture to the Indies?

Or think about Alexander Hamilton. From his harebrained military campaigns (in one case he led his men charging toward the opposition before the official signal was given to attack, a risky move that endangered lives but ultimately succeeded) to his equally wild political machinations, Hamilton displayed a brilliance that lay right at the border of the impractical—the hypomanic edge.

I would point out that like me, Gartner's goal is not to determine the most appropriate diagnostic label for his heroes. His point is not that these individuals would have benefited from antipsychotic medications and mood stabilizers. He is simply making the case that there are people who are genetically predisposed to high-energy behavior. Americans are particularly predisposed to this behavioral trait, and one could argue that it is an essential aspect of America's exceptional character.

Ascendant Strengths

A high-energy personality can be characterized by a number of positive characteristics, traits that you can learn to turn to your advantage. Here are some of the most common ascendant strengths:

ACHIEVEMENT When someone is "up," life seems to take a good turn and be awash in achievement. Dr. Sheri Johnson, a professor of psychology at the University of Miami, has conducted research studies that tell us more about how the symptoms of bipolar disorder affect people. The results hint that there is a connection between the manic aspect of bipolar and a person's drive to achieve. If it's true that even folks who have a diagnosable bipolar disorder can achieve a lot when their moods are elevated, perhaps we too—those of us who are not manic—can leverage our emotional upswings in the pursuit of our goals.

CONFIDENCE Mania and hypomania do seem to bring on upswings in confidence. In one study, Dr. Johnson and her team worked with a group of college students, first rating them on a hypomanic scale. Then the students were given a hand-eye coordination test. The students were told they had done well on the test, even if they hadn't. What came next is the interesting part. After the first test, the students were given a choice of tests they could take next. The hypomanic students, buoyed by their supposed success on the first one, typically chose a tougher test than did their nonmanic peers.[8]

RESILIENCE If you are inclined to hypomania, you have an underlying resilience, meaning you can respond to adversity with an increase in energy. This strength helps you bounce back when other people might collapse.

LIVELINESS You're lively. People find you fun to be around. You have tons of energy. You don't sleep much. You're upbeat and happy.

ENTHUSIASM Hypomania, in particular, is a heightened experience. It's something you want more of. You're fascinated by the world, and sometimes it seems that the world falls in love with you too.

CREATIVITY Both mania and hypomania contribute to creativity in many ways. They can heighten the imagination. They provide energy for creative activity. And, when in a state of depleted energy, the creative person can become inward-looking and find new sources of inspiration. It's like having a time-out, during which creativity can percolate.[9]

DRIVE One of the diagnostic symptoms for hypomania is an increase in goal-oriented behavior. People who are high on the bipolar continuum tend to be extremely focused and driven. They take on a challenge and they stick to it, channeling their high energy into achieving success.

BALANCING A HIGH-ENERGY LIFE

The challenge with high-energy living is finding balance without losing the energy and drive that make you unique. People with high-energy profiles tend to live life to the extreme—and that's a good thing. But making sure that you don't go over the edge, or drag others down with you, is important to maintaining a healthy, high-energy life.

Marc Peters told me about some of the tools he uses to maintain balance. When I spoke with Marc, he had just moved to a new state, where he will attend graduate school with the intention of earning a master's degree in public policy. He spoke about the challenges of reestablishing balance in a new environment.

One thing that Marc does to keep well balanced is to maintain regular eating and sleeping habits. Both high- and low-energy states can affect your lifestyle. During high-energy states, you might be tempted not to sleep at all, while during low-energy states you might find yourself falling into unhealthy eating habits. That's why people with the high-energy trait need to pay special attention to these daily habits.

It's not just about maintaining a healthy body. We all know that diet and rest are the two most important—and most often neglected—aspects of physical health. But we tend to forget that our mental health is affected by these things as well. If we don't eat right, and if we don't get enough rest, our bodies will get out of balance—and so will our minds.

In fact, recent studies have shown that sleep deprivation can be a major contributing factor to mental disorders. Doctors used to think that not sleeping was a symptom. Certainly, low levels of sleep can be symptomatic of hypomania, but as it turns out, reduced sleep also seems to trigger what psychiatrists refer to as "mood episodes." A longitudinal study of a thousand adults in Michigan found that individuals who suffer from a sleeping disorder were four times more likely to *develop* major depression. Other studies have found that depressed patients who experience insomnia are more likely than others to think about suicide than those who sleep normally.[10]

Scientists have found similar results for bipolar disorder. Not only does a lack of sleep seem to trigger manic episodes, but it can also make recovery more difficult.[11]

Along with balancing his eating, sleeping, and exercise habits, Marc works hard to maintain a strong social support system. Although it can be difficult, he makes sure to inform the important people in his life about his condition—he seeks out doctors he can rely on, and he speaks with his professors so that they can partner with him to maintain a healthy balance.

Even if you don't suffer from a disorder, keying people in to your own tendency toward shifting energy levels can be helpful. Colleagues and friends will be more understanding if you give them insight into your personality. Even if you are keenly aware that you have abruptly shifted from hyperactive to superslow, your change in behavior may leave the people in your life wondering.

The other thing that Marc does is keep a blog about his condition. This is part of the advocacy work that he does to spread awareness about bipolar disorder and to be a role model and mentor for people who feel, as he once did, that a bipolar life can't also be a successful life.

Blogging has been a really helpful tool for Marc in many ways. It helps his friends and family understand what he's going through. And, I would add, blogging or writing regularly is always a good opportunity to take a step back and see where you fall on that high-energy continuum—and to think about how you want to maximize the positive aspects of your current state.

High-Energy Living

One of the great things about the high-energy state is that people tend to be attracted to it. As I've said, when you're full of high energy, you are fun, enthusiastic, great to be around. Other people are drawn to your buoyant spirit.

At work, that attraction makes the high-energy state a great time to start new projects. Your natural charisma will draw other people in to your new initiatives. And your high energy—your creative thinking, focus, and passion—will help you put in the hours and creative thinking to go beyond your greatest expectations.

For example, Marc cofounded a new online initiative around gender equality when he was in a high-energy state. "I think someone who didn't have a hypomanic personality would start to think about all the different ways it wasn't going to work," Marc said. "But for me, because I'm in this place where I'm thinking big and thinking creative, I'm more focused on recognizing issues, working to address them right away, and looking for solutions."

High-energy states often come with an "I-can-do-it" attitude that helps you surpass boundaries that might hold other people back. I know that if my energy levels had been lower, I never would have attempted to live that crazy travel lifestyle for over a year. I would have said "That's impossible" and stayed home.

Instead, I took the plunge. And I found that my own abilities exceeded what society teaches us to expect from ourselves. That's the kind of healthy risk-taking that can come along with a high-energy profile.

Another place where a high-energy profile comes in handy is with relationships; a high-energy state can be a good time to meet someone new.

Marc admitted (a little shyly) that when he's feeling energetic, it often comes with a tendency to be more flirtatious than usual. High-energy states are marked by an increase in self-confidence. They can also come with an increase in sexual energy.

It's important to keep in mind, though, the risks that can come with a high-energy or hypomanic state. Many people are able to channel their hypomania into constructive activities—remember that drive is one of the ascendant strengths of this personality trait. But on the other hand, some people don't understand their trait well. They fall into the trap of irritability, impulsivity, and the desire for instant gratification—all things that high-energy folks are particularly vulnerable to. Alcohol and drug use, gambling, unsafe sex, and other risky behaviors can all result from an unfocused energy. If you understand how to control and channel this energy, however, you can use it to the good.

Another thing to consider if you are high on the bipolar continuum is that every period of high energy may come with a "recharge period" (the way mine does). If this is true for you, it's important to be aware of that impending shift. If you start a new project, or a new relationship, during a period of heightened energy, only to lose all interest a week later, then your colleagues and peers are bound to get frustrated. And so will you—it never feels good to let an initiative slide.

But if you are aware of the shift, you can plan around it. Before you start a new project, ask yourself whether it's something you're going to be able to maintain next week—and next month. Think carefully about your past history: Do you have a tendency to let projects drop? If you do, maybe you would be better off directing your high energy toward a project you already have in the works, or one that you're sure can be completed in a reasonable period of time. Temper your enthusiasm with self-awareness.

Prepare yourself, and the people around you, for the lows when they're on their way. If, like me, being alone is part of what you need to recharge, let the people around you know, especially a partner or spouse. Cancel your commitments in advance so you don't create a difficult situation for yourself.

If you do sometimes find yourself slipping during these periods from a state of restful contemplation to a state of frustration or unhappiness, then make sure (just as Marc does) that you have a support network you can fall back on, someone who can help you find a more positive state of mind, if not a more energetic one.

Remember the nature of your own energy cycles: You will be back up and doing great things again in no time.

Conclusion: Are You High Energy?

Where do you fall on the bipolar continuum? Do you tend to go through periods of intense energy and focus, what some people might call hypomanic periods? Do you sometimes push yourself past the edge of exhaustion and need to take some time to recharge?

I am high on the bipolar continuum so I sympathize with both the great strengths and the challenges of this particular personality trait. One of the most difficult aspects for me to come to terms with was the times when I was feeling down. It took me a long time to embrace this particular part of my personality. Instead, I judged myself harshly for being lazy or weak. It brought on a melancholy that was hard to shake. But now that I've learned to think of these times as periods for recharging my internal battery, I've come to enjoy the restful weekends that I spend by myself.

And those restful weekends are essential because they keep me from going past my limits during my hypomanic phases. If you're high on this continuum, you know that these periods of high energy, focus, creativity, and drive can be wonderfully inspiring. Many writers credit this feeling of elevated focus as an essential part of their writing process. I would imagine that people in many other professions feel the same. I know that this is the mental state in which I do my best work. Learning to understand and tap in to that energy will increase your creativity and drive. That's why bipolar is such an important trait to embrace.

NINE magical SCHIZOPHRENIA

OF THE EIGHT TRAITS in this book, *magical* is the most difficult to understand and explain, but also, I think, one of the most interesting and important.

What does it mean to be magical? One example of a magical individual is Benjamin Brafman, the lawyer who represented Sean Combs (aka Diddy, the rapper) in a 2001 gun possession trial. During that trial, Brafman wore a *bendel* (an Israeli bracelet thought to ward off the evil eye). Brafman won the trial (Diddy was acquitted), and since that day, although he doesn't believe in superstition, he has never taken it off. "I wear it because, since I've put it on, I've enjoyed good luck, both personally and professionally," he says. "Do I think about just breaking it off and throwing it away? Yes, the thought has occurred to me. But I haven't."[1]

Another example of magical thinking comes from my own experience as a poker player. Like many card players, I am a firm believer in gut instinct and I could often tell whether another player had a real hand (he was telling the truth) or was bluffing (he was lying). But sometimes it went further. There were times that I felt I could precisely name my opponent's hand, and I'd be right. Tapping in to the magical quality of my personality was part of the thrill of the game. Of course I wasn't "on" that way all the time. If I were, I might still be playing poker today.

Another example of a person with the magical trait is a friend and colleague from back in my home state: Nola Mae Ross. Nola Mae is an amazing woman. She has lived in southern Louisiana for all of her eighty-five years. For many years she ran a private airport with her husband, who was a pilot. When, sadly, he became afflicted with Alzheimer's and was unable to fly, Nola Mae had to give up the airport and take care of her husband full time. Or almost full time. She decided that she would take up writing in her spare moments.

Nola Mae found that her intuition, which she has always had plenty of, stood her in good stead as a writer. "I can pretty well figure people out ahead of time." When she was running the airport, she had an instinctive sense of when the pilots were going to be in danger, or when conflict might occur. Nola Mae has now written more than twenty-five books about the people and the land that she knows and loves. She says, "I was called to write," and she believes that. Listening to, and acting on, that calling was an act of faith—an act of magical thinking. Nola Mae is a six on the magical continuum.

Magical thinkers are flexible in their mind-sets, open-minded, self-confident, and intuitive. Almost all the successful people I profile in this book exhibit some level of magical thinking: Anyone who starts a new business, quits a job, goes on an adventure, or creates a work of art is acting, at least a little bit, on faith. That's fundamentally what magical thinking is.

Magical thinking gets complicated because it is often associated with other characteristics and behaviors, some of which are heavily stigmatized. Superstitions, for example—like the strange rituals that athletes sometimes engage in—are acts of magical thinking. One of these was the elaborate glove-adjusting routine that Nomar Garciaparra, longtime shortstop for the Boston Red Sox, would engage in before stepping into the batter's box. Another is NBA player LeBron James of the Miami Heat, who throws chalk dust into the air before every game. However, not all magical thinkers are superstitious.

And when I say that people with the magical trait often take actions on faith, I do not mean to imply that they are not grounded in reality. I am a person with religious faith, for example, and I believe in God, even though I have no quantitative proof that God exists. My ability to believe in something that is not tangible is in part due to my magical trait. And this is true of many other people.

Of course, one can place too much faith in the unknown to the point of being delusional—indeed, at the extreme of the magical continuum lies schizophrenia. I have worked with people at that end of the spectrum and I know how devastating the disorder can be. It must be seen with compassion and treated with a combination of therapeutic and medical care. Why compassion? Because any of us who know what it feels like to take a leap of faith is capable of understanding, at least to some degree, the struggle that comes with this disorder.

That's why I think this chapter is so important and has also been so difficult to write. First, I want to affirm the value of magical thinking to people in so many walks of life—from athletes to poker players to religious leaders to business innovators. And I do so as a professional whose work is based on the scientific model. Second, I want to argue that we should view those who suffer from genuine schizophrenia with the utmost compassion, as it is truly, without doubt, the most devastating of all the psychiatric disorders.

The Continuum Model: Magical

MAGICAL CONTINUUM				
RATIONAL		MAGICAL		SCHIZOPHRENIC
0	3	5	7	10+
Absent		Dominant		Superdominant

Here's how I think of the magical continuum.

If you are at the zero end of the continuum and have no signs of this trait at all, you live a highly rational life. You are extremely logical and ordered in your thinking. Your belief system and your decision-making process are based on facts that are themselves convincingly proven. (To you, anyway.) As I've said, schizophrenia lies at the other extreme, the ten end, and there is nothing to recommend that condition. But many people land in the middle, where magical thinking is a dominant trait. These people have faith and a strong sense of intuition.

Let me clarify further that the faith associated with magical thinking is not always the same as religious faith. In fact, some of the most confirmed atheists I know—even those with scientific backgrounds—have been known to take great leaps of faith or do things based almost solely on intuition. One great example is love. Falling in love is almost by definition an irrational act and often is an impractical or inconvenient endeavor. Yet every day thousands, possibly millions, of people—atheists, agnostics, and deep believers alike—find themselves falling head-over-heels in love.

Although magical thinking is not always a kind of religious faith, religious faith is typically a kind of magical thinking. Of course, there are people who have dedicated their lives to proving or disproving the existence of God through some scientific or logical process. But most of us who believe in a higher being (of whatever description) are "blind" in our belief. We may know there is a debate raging about the existence of God among intellectuals, but it doesn't really affect our faith. There's certainly some quantity of magic in that.

Moving along the continuum from conventional religious faith, we begin to encounter rarer forms of magical thinking, although still ones that do not create a cause for concern. Athletes, as we've seen, are famous for believing that certain rituals and actions will increase their chances of performing well or winning a game. But it's not just athletes. Many people believe that they are able to influence the future by performing personal rituals. Others believe in their powerful intuitive instincts—their ability to feel what other people are feeling or know what other people are thinking. My friend Lorraine, who is featured in the shyness chapter, told me that one of the reasons she dislikes being in groups is that she is able to feel what everyone around her is feeling. She has a heightened sense of empathy that makes social environments stressful.

Some people have an even more intense sense of intuition. While I, for example, believe I can sometimes predict the cards that other poker players are holding, some people believe they can listen in on other people's thoughts. A few actually believe they can hear the voice of God himself. It's not my role as a psychiatrist to determine whether it's possible to speak directly to God, so I'll make no further comment. Although, as I'll discuss later, my approach is to accept that just about anything is possible, even if we can't explain or understand it at this time.

I do know that for a small number of individuals (about 1 percent of the population), magical thinking ceases to be healthy, spiritual, or productive. These people break from reality entirely in their magical thinking. Their thought process becomes disordered—and this is where they reach the far end of the continuum and must be labeled as schizophrenic.

There is no way that schizophrenia is or can be a productive personality trait. But there is a sweet spot on this continuum where the right amount of magical thinking goes a long way toward making it possible for you to lead a happier, more productive, and more meaningful life. Learning to find and capitalize on that sweet spot is what this chapter is about.

Redefining Schizophrenia Spectrum Disorder

Here is an email exchange that I had with a woman named Stephanie on my website, DrDaleArcher.com.

Dear Dr. Archer,

My dad and grandmother were both schizophrenics. My father lost everything and became one of America's homeless when I was 14 years old and I had to help care for him. My way of coping was through my poetry. I never really fit in, and quite honestly I still don't. I have never had a relationship or kept a real job.

I am attempting to go to college at age 39. It has its ups and downs because I can't seem to remember anything I learn. I am pretending to be smart and somehow I am getting through it.

I will be honest and say that not many people know I also hear voices, and that I was diagnosed with schizoaffective disorder many years ago. I feel like there are spiritual aspects to schizophrenia, and I believe that until they study this aspect, no cure will be found. It is psychic warfare.

I was on the last show of MTV News Unfiltered *in 1999 with my father's story, and some people said I exploited my own father . . .*

Thank you for your time, Dr. Archer,

Stephanie

Dear Stephanie,

Thank you so much for writing. Yours is a very interesting story, filled not only with sorrow but also with hope.

Your father was very blessed to have you to care for him to the best of your ability. Many people talk about helping the mentally ill, but only a select few actually make a difference. You are one of the very few. As you so eloquently stated, society as a whole needs to look at their little children and realize that one day their little darling might be one of the homeless mentally ill.

Until we stop making it someone else's problem, situations like your father's will remain the way they are. You are on the right road to making a very big change in how we view the mentally ill and what we can do to help them.

One note about you hearing voices and schizophrenia. I agree that there are certain cases of what I call "magical thinking" that don't need to be treated if the individual is able to function in life. These very thoughts you have may contribute to your creativity.

However, you state that you don't have a job, and thus you may want to consider a psychiatric evaluation and a trial of medication to see if it helps. . . . I wish you much success in your endeavors.

Dr. Archer

Hi Dr. Archer,

I had to think this over before I could reply. I'm Stephanie, the one who wrote the letter. Thanks for replying. It was nice of you and though I do think the mentally ill need their medications at times, I wish you would open your mind to the fact that many are being tormented by spirits....

Stephanie, I try to keep an open mind about all things, as I think anything is possible. Thanks for checking in again and giving a unique viewpoint.

I hope that this dialogue between Stephanie and me helps to reveal some of the complexity underlying any conversation about the magical continuum. My point in including this story is that I do not wish to make judgments about these conditions. Rather, I want to illustrate a different way of thinking and talking about schizophrenia, and about magical thinking as well.

So let's talk a bit more about what schizophrenia is and how it is different from magical thinking. At its most extreme, schizophrenia is the most devastating disorder in the DSM. Diagnostic symptoms of schizophrenia include delusions, hallucinations, disorganized speech, grossly disorganized or catatonic behavior, alogia (the inability to speak), and avolition (a lack of initiative or goals).

It's easy to see why schizophrenia is so heavily stigmatized in the United States: We are comfortable with people being highly energetic, adventurous, or even obsessive, but delusions and hallucinations don't fit easily into the scientific, fact-based way of thinking that we prefer and so admire. Furthermore, unlike the symptoms of ADHD, which are fairly prevalent in our society and, as we've seen, don't always indicate pathology (e.g., fidgets often; has trouble paying attention), schizophrenia's telltale signs can seem foreign, bizarre, and scary to anyone unfamiliar with this disorder. I hope that as you come to understand the links between schizophrenia and magical thinking, some of this fear will fade away.

The stigma toward those with schizophrenia is made worse by the perception that it is a violent illness. This perception may arise from portrayals in movies, television, and novels of people whose paranoid delusions lead them to take violent action. These fictional portrayals come to mind when similar violent actions occur in real life. People were quick to speculate, for example, that Jared Loughner—the gunman who went on a shooting spree in Tucson in January 2011—might suffer from schizophrenic delusions. When it turned out that he did, it only reinforced the stigma.

The fact is that schizophrenia *is* occasionally accompanied by violence, but most people who suffer from the disorder are not violent. To put it in perspective, individuals diagnosed with schizophrenia are less likely to be violent than those with affective disorder, substance abuse disorder, or a personality disorder. As one group of researchers studying the issue wrote, "It would seem that public fear of persons with schizophrenia living in the community is largely unwarranted, though not totally groundless."[2]

Above all, it's important to understand that schizophrenia is treatable and that antipsychotic medications can help people manage the troubles—such as delusions, hallucinations, and scrambled thinking—that often come along with the disorder. And there is new hope that people with schizophrenia can also be helped with a form of talk therapy, usually in conjunction with medication. Researchers at the University of Pennsylvania developed a program designed to help people with schizophrenia set very specific goals—such as "going out for coffee, visiting a local bookshop, or volunteering at a community center"—and work slowly toward achieving them. Success with one small goal can give patients the strength and sense of mastery that enables them to try achieving another one. The thirty-one people who took part in the study showed significantly more improvement in their condition than those who received medications alone.[3] Stay tuned on this one. Whatever the best treatment may be, it's absolutely essential that these folks get the support and care they need.

But even when people diagnosed with schizophrenia do receive therapy and appropriate meds, the social stigma remains so strong that it can inhibit them from functioning with any kind of normalcy. In fact, the stigma is so real and potent that some psychiatrists refer to it as a "second disorder." The way we as a society conceive of mental disorders has a huge impact on the mental health of disordered patients. By understanding what magical thinking is, why it occurs, and what happens when it becomes debilitating, we can embrace our own magical thinking and improve the lives of those who struggle with schizophrenia.

An Evolutionary Imperative

The question of *why* schizophrenia exists is such a puzzling one that it has earned its own name among psychiatrists: the schizophrenia paradox.

The problem is one we've encountered before, in other chapters. Schizophrenia occurs in about 1 percent of the population worldwide. It has a polygenic basis, meaning that there is no single "schizophrenia gene." It is associated with a number of different genes, in combination with environmental factors. Its symptoms—which include delusions, auditory hallucinations, and loss of coherence in thought and language—often begin to appear with puberty. It is known to have a marked impact on a person's fecundity (number of children).[4]

Furthermore, schizophrenia seems to have been around for a long time. People with schizophrenia have been identified in every culture in the world, and the prevalence rate is consistent globally. Even Australian Aborigines, whose genetic material has been isolated for sixty thousand years, suffer from schizophrenia. That means schizophrenia is probably more than sixty thousand years old—and many scientists think it's a lot older than that.[5]

So how did schizophrenia survive for so many thousands of years? Why has natural selection selected schizophrenia? There are many possibilities that researchers have considered. Genetics is a new science and the study of evolution is hardly conclusive.

To imagine one possible benefit of the schizophrenia genes, picture yourself back in a Stone Age village about sixty thousand years ago, which is when the first anthropological evidence of religion appears. Along with religion came the belief in nonphysical beings—some form of deity or god. And along with belief in these beings came the belief that there were certain unique individuals who were capable of communicating with the supernatural. These shamans were sacred individuals, the spiritual guides of the Stone Age village.

Interestingly, there are many parallels between shamanic behavior and schizophrenia. Shamanic powers tend to originate at puberty, which is the same time that schizophrenic symptoms first start to appear. Shamanic visions are similar to the hallucinations experienced by people with schizophrenia. And the prevalence rate of schizophrenia (about one per every hundred people) is about the same as the prevalence of shamans in today's tribal societies. So it's possible that there is a genetic link between shamanism and schizophrenia—that today's schizophrenics share genetic material with the shamans, prophets, and sacred leaders of the past.

This theory was popular with anthropologists in the 1960s and 1970s. Although it has fallen out of fashion in recent decades, I think there is good reason to reinvoke the relationship between shamanism and schizophrenia. It helps explain why magical thinking is such a valuable asset in today's society, just as it has been for thousands of years.

Another exciting new possibility that scientists have been exploring is that perhaps the genes associated with schizophrenia are also associated with certain *positive* personality traits such as creativity, imagination, intelligence, and openness to experience. Studies in the last decade have found that certain genes associated with increased risk of schizophrenia (genes with names such as COMT, HTR2A, SLC6A4, etc.) have in fact been associated with these positive traits among the psychologically healthy population.[6]

If you have some of these genes, you are likely to exhibit certain positive personality traits. If you have all of them, *and if the environmental factors are right,* you may develop schizophrenia. This is definitely a continuum trait.

Actually, this research points to the genetic basis that underlies my continuum model of behavioral traits. The point is that people who have a few "schizophrenia genes" might be exceptionally creative, imaginative, intelligent, and open to experience. This has been shown to be true particularly among families of people with schizophrenia. These people share genes with their more disabled family members. But instead of being a ten on the continuum (i.e., schizophrenic), they are a six or a seven. They're magical thinkers.

This isn't to say, however, that all people with magical personalities, or their children, are at risk of schizophrenia. The genetic and environmental factors that lead to schizophrenia are so complex that no one can say for certain where and when the disorder will be present. It is hoped more research in neuroscience and genetics will help us better understand this disorder and find new ways of helping schizophrenic individuals move away from the unhealthy end of the continuum toward a more healthy and productive state of magical thinking, that sweet spot on the magical continuum.

Whether you are interested in this trait because you are a magical thinker yourself, or because you are one of a growing number of people interested in finding new ways to think about schizophrenia, I hope the continuum model will help you embrace your magical trait and better understand that of others.

Ascendant Traits

The positive aspects of the magical trait include:

IMAGINATION Maybe your parents called you a daydreamer or your teachers thought of you as a space cadet, but it's important to remember that some form of daydreaming or imaginative thinking is usually involved in the creation of new things, whether it's a technological innovation or a work of art.

INTELLIGENCE Studies suggest that many schizophrenic individuals come from families with above-average IQs. In an age where all professions require more and more knowledge and technical skill, your exceptional intelligence should put you ahead of the curve.

INTUITION Some people can sense what others are thinking and feeling; others can identify a good move in poker or on the stock market. But knowing how and when to go with your gut can lead to great opportunities.

FAITH The physical and mental health benefits of faith are enormous. As a faithful person, your confidence in other people helps in your personal and professional relationships. The confidence that you show in your coworkers and colleagues helps you to be an effective team player (maybe that's why so many athletes are magical thinkers!). And in your personal life, your friends and loved ones sense that you trust them implicitly, and they will return that trust.

Those who have religious faith tend to feel more optimistic and hopeful about the future than those who do not believe. They are better able to find meaning in their lives.[7] And a positive relationship with God has been shown to improve a person's mental health.[8] It has even been found that schizophrenic individuals who suffer from religious delusions are also able to use religion to help in their recovery.[9]

Of course, if you have religious faith, it's not because science says it will reduce your risk of mental health disorders by some percentage. Your faith is an honest belief in God, and I acknowledge that. I leave it up to you to decide what role God plays in the positive benefits that faith has on your life.

A MAGICAL LIFE

I'd like to bring you back with me to 2004, when I played in the main event at the World Series of Poker in Las Vegas.

It was the final year that the tournament was played at Binion's Horseshoe, the historic hotel where the tournament was founded forty years ago. The smell of mildew was so strong in my room that I had to keep the window open the entire week. The noise from the casino and the lights from the street outside kept me awake at night.

But what can I say? I'm a magical thinker. I have always believed that you should "stay where you play." I remember that I knew that I was there to win. Self-confidence against all odds is characteristic of magical thinkers.

There is one moment in particular that I want to describe to you. It was 2:30 in the morning on the third day of the tournament and I had been playing since noon. You could say I wasn't at my best. We were about to play the final hand of the night.

I had been playing very conservatively the whole tournament. I'm not sure what happened that night—maybe I was too tired to think straight, or maybe I had convinced myself that the sooner I won this last hand the sooner I'd be able to go up to my mildewy room and fall into bed.

But things took a downturn on the last hand of the night. My rational, scientific mind told me that I should just give up the pot and play again tomorrow. My chances of winning were minuscule, and there were a lot of chips on the line. But just before I folded, a powerful feeling came over me and I knew, *knew*, that I was going to win this hand. I know all of you skeptics out there are screaming right now, but what can I say? It was a magical-thinking moment, and I couldn't resist it. Instead of making the rational decision and folding, I went all in, betting every chip I had.

If I'd coolly considered the odds, I knew I had little chance of winning and that my ability to stay in the tournament depended on the two cards to come. In fact, I had an 85 percent chance of losing all of my chips and busting out.

And then, bam! I drew the card I needed. I won the hand and busted my opponent. My friend and accomplished pro poker player David Williams had been watching and told me in no uncertain terms that what I had done was nuts.

Of course he was totally right.

Here's the thing: It doesn't matter if you believe in magic, and it doesn't matter that I can't rationally explain what happened to me that night. If I had played logically in that hand, I would have folded. Maybe it was magic, and maybe it was luck—I say it doesn't matter. What matters is this: When you know, you know. If any of you have ever had that feeling, then you will know exactly what I'm talking about.

My point here is not that every magical thinker should be a poker player. But magical thinkers excel at taking a well-timed risk, making a leap of faith, and sometimes winning big as a result. That's something that you can use to your advantage no matter what kind of decisions you're making—whether you're deciding to start your own business, move to a new city, or ask someone out on a first date.

As this story illustrates, magical thinking is quite complex. On the one hand, in certain situations, magical thinking—the belief that things will work out your way—will make it possible for you to make decisions others might balk at. If you work in a field dependent on creativity and innovation, it might backfire sometimes, but if it works out, the gains can be enormous.

However, let me add a word of caution. Risking everything in that poker game was a worthwhile bet for me at the time. It was similar to the risk I took a few years later when I decided to shift away from my full-time career in clinical psychiatry. Both were risks that I could afford to take. I risked losing the tournament in that poker hand, but I wasn't going to lose my house or my car. And if my media endeavors hadn't worked out, I always had my psychiatric practice to fall back on. Both decisions were mine alone and bore few consequences for other people in my life. But if I had made the decision to move to New York fifteen years earlier, when my wife at the time and young kids were still dependent on me, it would have been a very different decision with very different potential consequences all around.

Magical thinkers do sometimes have a tendency to take high risks even when they are not in a good position to do so. So if you are a magical thinker, and are often moved by instinct, make sure you check that instinct against your priorities. If you are risking something that is important to you, like your family, then think again.

Let your magical thinking be a guiding light in your life. Just make sure that you're not following it blindly.

WORKING FOR OTHERS

Magical thinkers are well suited to jobs and activities that involve working with other people. Empathy, intuition, and faith lead magical thinkers toward careers where they can help people—as educators or religious leaders, through social work, or even as writers.

Consider once again my friend Nola Mae Ross. Along with an enjoyable collection of ghost stories and mysteries, Nola Mae has written two books about hurricanes that struck the area around Lake Charles, Louisiana, where I'm from. Research for the books required interviewing hundreds of survivors and their families. "When I started writing," Nola Mae said, "I thought: I can't do this." Her first interview was with a woman whose home had flooded during Hurricane Audrey, which hit the area in 1957. She had hoisted her two young children onto the top of a cabinet to keep them above the rising waters, then the house collapsed. She never saw her children again. "I thought, well this is just too sad," Nola Mae said. "But I went ahead and I talked to the woman."

That courage in the face of emotional adversity—a courage that is based in her personal faith and sense of social responsibility—is a sign of magical thinking. Nola Mae saw the same kind of courage and resilience among the hurricane survivors she interviewed. Her books are in part a tribute to that survival instinct.

In order to represent the voices of these tragic and inspiring stories, Nola Mae had to tap in to her own natural empathy. "My intuition and spirituality allowed me to feel what my subjects were feeling," she said. Once she got in touch with those feelings, it became easier for her to translate the tales into writing. I would add that it made her a uniquely appropriate voice for these deeply touching and human stories.

I'd also add that magical thinkers tend to be quite expressive and can be highly successful as writers or artists. Maybe it's the unique perspective on life that a magical mind can provide, or maybe it's the openness to new ideas and new possibilities that magical thinkers tend to possess. But Nola Mae Ross is just one of many writers who tends toward the magical.

Another person who has used his magical thinking to help people through writing is Neale Donald Walsch, author of the well-known Conversations with God series. As Walsch describes it, he was in a period of despair and frustration when he turned to God for guidance. To his surprise, God answered back—leading to a series of sometimes profound, and often inspiring, written conversations. The conversations—which deal frankly with such topics as life challenges, geopolitical and metaphysical life on the planet, and universal truths about the opportunities of the soul—have inspired countless people.

Of course, these conversations have also inspired controversy. Walsch claims to have spoken directly with God. Is his claim honesty or heresy? Is his experience sacred or psychotic? That's not for me to judge or decide. As a psychiatrist, I can say that Walsch is clearly not suffering from a debilitating mental illness—he is not suffering, and he is not debilitated. If anything, he has found purpose and meaning in his life through this unusual experience.

As for the validity of this claim, I'll let Walsch justify it himself. The first question he poses is this: "How can I know this communication is from God? How do I know this is not my own imagination?"

Here is the answer he receives: "*What would be the difference?* Do you not see that I could just as easily work through your imagination as anything else? I will bring you the *exact* right thoughts, words, or feelings, at any given moment, suited precisely to the purpose at hand, using one device, or several.

"You will know these words are from Me because you, of your own accord, have never spoken so clearly. Had you already spoken so clearly on these questions, you would not be asking them."[10]

MAGICAL THINKING AND COPING

In her heartbreaking book *The Year of Magical Thinking,* Joan Didion describes how her form of magical thinking—beliefs that are separated from reality—made it possible for her to cope with an unbearable circumstance. Her husband died suddenly and unexpectedly one evening while the two were having dinner in their New York apartment. Almost unbelievably, Didion's daughter fell into a coma that same day. Didion credits her capacity for magical thinking for keeping her sane and alive. Her book, and the stage play that was based upon it, is a beautifully wrought tale of magical thinking at the edge of despair.

Magical thinking is often credited with helping people work through such deep and wrenching struggles. Faith and religion both serve as mental and emotional support systems for individuals struggling with their own mental health.

One example of this is my friend Lorraine, the shy woman whom I described in detail in an earlier chapter. Lorraine struggled for years with alcoholism, and I related how her inner strength enabled her to eventually get sober. But Lorraine is also a magical thinker, and that magical thinking affects her life and her sobriety. In our interview, she described her heightened sense of empathy. "It just seems to me like when I get around people and they're bad people or thinking bad thoughts, it rubs off on me."

You may remember that Lorraine said this was one of the reasons she couldn't go to AA meetings. She could feel how much everyone present was struggling and she found it overwhelming, not just because she doesn't like big groups of people, but because her heightened empathy made her aware of all the misery in the room. On the other hand, she says, "If I go to church I definitely catch a positive and much more uplifting mood."

Lorraine's magical thinking may have kept her away from AA, but it was also key to her recovery—she gives the most credit for her recovery to God. "I do a lot of praying," she said. "I do know I had help from above."

In addition to prayer, Lorraine used self-hypnosis, a technique that taps in to the power of suggestion to implant ideas about everything from smoking and drinking to weight loss. Hypnosis is a practice that depends in part on faith—its effectiveness comes from your ability to believe in it. Lorraine's magical thinking made it possible for her to do so.

Nola Mae also spoke about the power of magical thinking in helping people get through difficult times. During her hurricane research, she uncovered incredible stories of survival and rebuilding in the face of great tragedy. "It wasn't just tragedy," Nola Mae said. "There was an awful lot of courage and bravery, a lot of humor, and a lot of spirituality." Faith in God and in each other, along with a sometimes astonishing sense of optimism, allowed people to rebuild after Hurricane Audrey.

"They believed that even though this was happening, God was still in control," Nola Mae said. "The people immediately dug back in and rebuilt and did everything they could to help themselves. My dad took bulldozers and equipment and helped them move trash. Everybody in the nearby towns that could went down and helped."

In fact, Nola Mae thinks that magical thinking is one of the characteristics of the Cajun culture that dominates southern Louisiana, which she describes as strong, freedom-loving, and resilient. I don't know whether magical thinking is part of the genetic makeup of the Cajun community. But we can see how magical thinking has helped this oft-beleaguered group of people survive and even thrive across Louisiana.

Magical Thinking and Relationships

Love is the area of our lives where we are all the most vulnerable to magical thinking. How do we know when we've met "the one"? Why do we believe that there is "one" person for us? Does love, as an objective or scientifically verifiable experience, even exist?

Some people credit love to pheromones, chemicals that in many animals are thought to attract mates. But most of us think of love as something far more ephemeral and hard to pin down—a truly magical experience.

Do you believe in love at first sight? If so, when it comes to love, then you're a magical thinker.

Don't worry, though, you're not alone. Magical love stories—and the magical potions and rituals associated with them—have been around for centuries, if not millennia. In ancient Greece, the sirens were dangerous bird-women who seduced nearby sailors with their enchanting voices. They used the magic of seduction in order to bring sailors to their death.

Love potions—all manners of ritual and chemical tricks for winning someone's affection—are another ancient form of magical thinking. In Shakespeare's *A Midsummer Night's Dream,* love potions go awry when the fairy Puck sprinkles a love potion into the eyes of Titania, the queen of the fairies. The potion curses her to fall in love with the first creature she sees—in this case, a foolish peasant whose head has been transformed into that of a donkey.

Things get even more complicated when Puck interferes with human relationships. Intending to help out Helena, a lovelorn maiden in distress, he uses the potion to make the object of her affections (Demetrius) fall in love with her. But in a case of mistaken identities he uses the potion on the wrong man! Now two couples are in a state of disarray.

But by the end of the play, everything is in its correct order. A love-potion antidote fixes the havoc that Puck has caused, and some judiciously applied elixer brings Helena and Demetrius together at last. Magical thinking saves the day. But in the end, it's love that triumphs.

The myth of a potion that can cure unrequited love is one that is strong to this day. In the book (and subsequent film) *Like Water for Chocolate,* a young couple is kept apart by the rules of their traditional Mexican family. The power of their love is so strong that it seeps into everything they do. It gets into the food prepared for a wedding feast, causing the entire wedding party to get "sick with love." The young woman's lovesickness eventually becomes so strong that it burns down an entire house. And in the 2000 movie *Chocolat,* the heroine wins the love of the citizens of a conservative French village (and Johnny Depp) with the power of her chocolate.

You may be thinking that magical love stories belong in the realms of movies and Greek mythology. But I know of one young woman who actually used a ritual to call her future husband to her. "I did everything I could think of," she explained. "I held a ritual with candles and prayers."

Sounds a bit unusual, sure. But here are some of the other rituals that this young woman tried: speed dating and online dating. As it turned out, she met her husband the old-fashioned way, at a dinner party. But, she says, "I don't think we would have met if I hadn't tried every possible solution."

Is online dating an act of faith? I think so. But that's only because all dating is somehow opening your mind to the possibility that two strangers could in fact be "meant" to spend the rest of their lives together. It's hard to believe in, and yet so many of us do. That's surely magical thinking.

An interesting thing happens when magical thinkers actually get involved in a relationship. Throughout this book I've been standing by the statement *Opposites attract.* But it turns out that magical thinkers are the wild card when it comes to matchmaking. Magical thinkers can be successful in relationships with people regardless of their dominant trait, from OCD to narcissism.

Why are magical thinkers so flexible? Intuition and empathy can help them understand their partners better. Faith makes it easier for a magical thinker to establish trust, which is essential for a long-term, successful partnership.

But I think the key is faith in love itself. Cynical folks are likely to end a relationship before it even begins because they are hyperaware of the factors that are working against them. (Statistics about divorce rates are evidence that any decent cynic might use to give up on love altogether.) But magical thinkers have faith that despite the odds, their relationships will work. As long as they are willing to put in the effort to keep their faith alive, magical thinkers are a step or two ahead of the rest of us when it comes to relationships.

CONCLUSION: ARE YOU MAGICAL?

Where do you fall on the magical continuum? Complete the questionnaire in the back of this book, and then mark your spot on the continuum. Then think about your friends, your family, your colleagues. Are you the most magical person in your world? Or the most rational among your peers?

Magical thinking can be associated with risky behaviors, impulsive decision making, and sometimes, choices that less-magical people find difficult to understand. If you tend toward any of these things, take some time to think about how you can make changes to keep your magical thinking from getting in your way. Especially if you sometimes make risky or impulsive decisions, make sure you maintain a list in your mind of the things that are most important to you in a given situation. Don't let yourself sacrifice the big things in life for a small win.

Then think about the positive aspects of this trait. Magical thinking can give meaning to our lives. It can help us behave intuitively in complex situations. Its ascendant strengths include imagination, intelligence, intuition, and faith. If you are a magical thinker, I can only advise you to embrace these strengths! We may live in a rational world, but excessive rationality just leads to paralysis in daily life. So become comfortable trusting your inner intuition. Let your imagination roam. Embracing your trait of magical thinking may be the path to a happier and more meaningful life.

CONCLUSION

On March 9, 2011, the *New York Times* ran an article about the state of psychiatry today. As the article describes it, the typical psychiatric practice has become little more than a drug dispensary. Patients come in to a psychiatrist's office and fifteen minutes later they exit with a prescription for a mood-altering medication, such as an antidepressant or an anti-anxiety med.[1]

"I'm concerned that I may be put in a position where I'd be forced to sacrifice patient care to make a living," says one student of psychiatry who is quoted in the article. The student, like many psychiatrists, blames the health insurance industry for the problem, because payment policies make it more lucrative for a psychiatrist to write a prescription than to give therapy. Others blame the DSM, which is responsible for defining who is sick (and in need of medication) and who is not. And still others blame the pharmaceutical industry, which is in the business of making money by creating medicines that treat and manage people's sicknesses rather than preventing or curing them.

It's my view that psychiatrists, health insurers, and pharmaceutical companies must all take some responsibility for our current situation. The unfortunate result of their collective pursuit of power and financial gain is a society in which every person with an emotional problem is sent through a medical assembly line where a diagnosis is slapped on them, they're prescribed a medication or two, and sent on their way. The whole process may take forty-five minutes for a first-time visitor, and fifteen minutes for the repeat customer—sorry, I mean *patient.*

What we end up with is an overdiagnosed, overmedicated, and undertreated society. Medications work well when they are carefully prescribed to people whose severe symptoms interfere with their daily functioning, whose problems cannot be resolved by lifestyle changes alone. That was the case with Marc Peters, who appeared in chapter 8, about the bipolar continuum.

But most of us are fortunate not to have severe symptoms such as psychosis, delusions, or suicidal thoughts. Most of us struggle with something much more pervasive: We are distinctively shaped pegs trying to fit ourselves into uniform holes. We are faced with difficult challenges at work and at home. We get hired, get fired, move from one job to another. We move to new homes, start families, lose loved ones. In other words, we live through the full range of human experience.

In the end we are all much alike and life is very simple. It's just not very easy. But if we give everyone who's struggling a diagnosis and shove a tablet down his or her throat, we make a huge mistake. Marc described how, after he was diagnosed with bipolar disorder, he became severely depressed because he thought that there was no place in the world for people with his condition. He thought he had to give up on all of his dreams because he sometimes experiences such severe symptoms.

That is simply not true. And it demonstrates how a diagnosis can be totally debilitating rather than helpful and curative. A diagnosis can sometimes help doctors figure out an appropriate course of treatment. But it can also cause a patient to give up hope and stop pursuing the kind of satisfaction in life that everyone wants and deserves.

The truth is that Marc, without the help of his meds, is a ten-plus on the bipolar continuum. His meds probably help him adjust down to an eight, which means that he still has a hypomanic personality. And when I look at the successes he has already achieved, I see no reason why he should be forced to be classified in a way that carries a lot of stigma with it. What I see instead is a young man who has developed a high level of awareness about his dominant personality trait, its accompanying challenges, and its ascendant traits. And I see someone who has used that awareness to better pursue his dreams.

If you've learned one thing from this book, I hope it's that for most of us, good mental health comes from embracing who you are in every area of your life. You should know by now which personality traits are dominant for you and for your loved ones. I hope you also understand how maximizing those traits—and the ascendant strengths that go with them—will help you lead a happier and more fulfilling life.

We all have a unique personality profile. When we truly know ourselves, we let that uniqueness shine. Furthermore, it is only when we truly know ourselves that we can tap in to our dominant personality traits to achieve greater happiness and success in all aspects of our lives, from our working lives to our relationships with our family and our loved ones.

I think of my own career. It took me years to find a profession that would allow me to fully embrace my histrionic personality (my love of the spotlight), my high energy, and my ADHD. Every time I went on a solo sail or took a cross-country motorcycle trip, I was finding an outlet for an adventurous spirit that was suppressed much of the time.

Today I find that my schedule and location are often unpredictable. Last week I found myself in Los Angeles, shooting a pilot for an upcoming television show. Then it was back to Lake Charles and my psychiatric clinic. Next it's on to New York, where I'm writing blog posts and appearing on television to talk about Charlie Sheen. (Where do you think he falls on the bipolar continuum or the narcissistic one?) Every week brings a different topic, a different challenge, a different location. It's thrilling to really let my ADHD personality loose.

I'm not the only one who has gone down a long and winding path in search of the profession that's right for my profile. Remember Kurt, who abandoned his academic aspirations after earning a Ph.D. because he realized he was too OCD to be a writer? He has now found a better place for himself as a precision machinist.

Or think of Lorraine, the shy woman who spent years working in a cubicle for a horrendous boss because she wanted to be a lawyer. It took a long time, but quitting that job and becoming an independent practitioner who can work from home was the best thing she ever did.

If you're just starting out on your career path, like Seth, the young man on the ADHD continuum who is traveling the world, or Alexis, the young woman with OCD traits who works in event planning, I hope you can take some inspiration from these stories. You do not need to spend years suppressing your true identity. If you take the time now to get to know yourself, you'll find it easy to recognize when you're in a place that's just not right for you. And it may not happen overnight, but you can move toward aligning your personality with your lifestyle. You can achieve a professional life that's perfectly suited to your identity.

Of course, as you get older and your life changes, your needs, your dreams, and even your personality will change too. Right now Seth is an eight on the ADHD continuum, content to travel the world. But what will happen if he wants to have a family? Or if he starts dreaming of establishing roots in one of the hundreds of countries he's visited?

Seth may find that other personality traits become more dominant as his priorities change. That's why it's important that you continue to check in with yourself and reevaluate your personality profile. It should come as no surprise that a great job when you're twenty might cease to satisfy you when you're forty-five. But if Seth, in deciding to settle down and have a family, ignores his ADHD personality altogether, he will ultimately regret it. I guarantee that his wanderlust will never truly fade. That's why, even if he does decide to settle down geographically, I would advise him to find a way to keep his ADHD trait alive.

Leonard is an example of someone whose dominant trait has changed a great deal over time. When he was young, his anxiety worked well for him (he was an A student, went to a prestigious law school, got a great job on graduation), but it came at a price. His social life suffered, and he wasn't happy. As he got older, the combination of anxiety, stress, and social dissatisfaction pushed his anxiety up the continuum until it became unbearable. If your anxiety is giving you panic attacks so severe you feel like you're dying, it's probably time to take a good look at your life and make some changes.

Which is exactly what Leonard did. Now he works hard and plays hard, particularly with his kids. He may not have been a partyer in college, but partying was probably never a priority for him. This is not the case when it comes to his kids.

Other important lifestyle changes that Leonard made include more exercise, healthier eating habits, and yoga. These are changes that we can all consider if we feel that one of our traits is becoming overwhelming.

You may remember that in the ADHD chapter, Seth declared it was hard to find someone whose personality profile matched his. In the short term, he might think that he needs someone who is as adventurous and unpredictable as he is. But in fact, the general advice I give to people worried about their relationships is the tried-and-true fact that opposites attract. People who are high in one profile tend to do well with someone who is high in a different, but complementary, trait. That was certainly the case with Alexis, whose OCD traits matched perfectly with those of her ADHD boyfriend (although she confessed that the attraction was mysterious even to her). Or Leora, the histrionic young woman whose boyfriend is a scientist, and who falls at about two or three on the histrionic continuum. Her ability to express her emotions keeps the relationship honest and intimate, while his emotional stability keeps things grounded. They balance each other.

Leora and Alexis are both in their twenties, but the pattern holds for longer-lasting relationships. I remember the story that Kurt told about how he makes shopping decisions. He does all the research, looks up all the product stats, and gathers the data. Then his wife takes the basic information he can provide, goes out, and makes the purchase. When real, detailed information is necessary, Kurt is able to provide it. But when his OCD trait becomes paralyzing, his wife steps in and makes a decision.

And here's an interesting thing: After Kurt was interviewed for this book, he spoke with his wife about his OCD trait. He hadn't expected the discussion to have long-term implications. But according to his wife, it actually changed the dynamics of their relationship! "I always thought that we were in a decision-making process together," she explained. "But now I realize that he's just a paralyzed person, and he won't be offended if I help him move forward." She says it has made planning for their upcoming vacation a thousand times easier. I hope that understanding your profile can have a similar impact on your life.

At the end of the interview with Nola Mae Ross, she spoke about life's challenges. "I lost two sons, nine or ten years apart," she said. "One was seventeen, and one was twenty-nine. I lost three husbands and yet I think I've had a very happy and good life."

What an inspiring thing to say. I think that's something that we can all hope for. "I've had experiences that might have knocked me down sometimes," she said. That's something that, unfortunately, we can all expect. And that's why it's so important that we stay so strong in terms of who we are and how we feel about ourselves. In

Nola Mae's case, that meant embracing her magical thinking. "I think it's my faith that brought me through all of this," she said.

When I first had the idea for this book, it just clicked. Just as I *knew* I would win the poker hand that I described in the chapter on magical thinking, I *knew* that I was on to something with this topic. I deeply believe that there's a link between the qualities that make us great and the categories of mental health defined by the DSM. I know from research and experience that these qualities, or traits, fall on a continuum. And I have seen that by learning to embrace your traits, you can come to live a better, more satisfying life.

Since I first conceived of the book, I've spent a lot of time thinking about and developing these ideas. Although I began by considering just seven traits, I subsequently added an eighth, narcissistic. That's because I realized that some of the great public figures whom I most admire are motivated more by self-confidence than by a love of performance. Clearly their greatness wasn't defined just by a histrionic nature. Their narcissism, or self-focus, was much more central.

I've also had the opportunity to test my ideas about these traits on my friends and family and in my clinic. With one of my colleagues, Dr. Jerry Whiteman, I ran a study to put my theories to the test. I wanted to see how people responded to the eight traits. The questionnaires in the back of this book are one result of that study.

In the course of our research, we noticed an interesting trend. Many of the people we studied had just one or two dominant traits. A smaller number of the participants, however, possess several of the traits and rank toward the ten end on many of them. I'm a good example of this. I'm seven or higher on the continuums for four traits: narcissistic, histrionic, ADHD, and bipolar, and a six on magical. Dietrich, the serial entrepreneur who appeared in the ADHD and narcissism chapters, is the same way. When he was interviewed, he said that he had almost all the same traits that I have, with anxiety to boot. (That trait, he joked, comes from his Jewish mother.)

These folks run high on the continuums, so I call them "high-traited." As it turns out, there are certain trends among us high-traited people. Dietrich and I are both high-traited *performers*. We love being in the spotlight and our combination of dominant traits—narcissism, histrionic, adventurous—makes us perfectly suited for the position.

Other high-traited individuals are our exact opposite—they are high on the OCD, social anxiety, and generalized anxiety continuums. This should make intuitive sense—these folks are hyperfocused, driven, and independent. They have a different set of traits from the performers. But like me and Dietrich, they have strong dominant traits that combine to make a powerful personality profile.

And then there are the people who are low across the board. These low-traited folks are threes and fours on their most dominant traits. They may say that they're a little bit shy, or that they sometimes get anxious, but in general these people are pretty low key for every trait.

It's not surprising that our preliminary data show that high-traited and low-traited folks make great partners. Whether it's marriage or professional partnership, these types complement each other. While low-traited people are flexible and easygoing, high-traited people bring focus and drive. While two high-traited people may seem to form a pair that is full of lively energy at first, they tend to burn out (or burst into flames) early on. Mild-mannered pairs risk fading into boredom. Pairs that complement each other, on the other hand, stay stable longer. It's the same pattern that I identified for each of the traits—the old story of "opposites attract" brought to light in a new way.

I plan to continue gathering data on the eight traits. If you learn something interesting about yourself from this book, I encourage you to get in touch with me—the best way is to visit my website, DrDaleArcher.com. Stories of people like you and me help explain and clarify these traits and the way they interact. Is your dominant trait affected by your spouse's trait? How do your traits change over time? How can understanding the eight traits help couples, groups, or offices work better together?

As more and more people take these questionnaires, a wealth of knowledge about human personalities will be revealed.

At the end of his interview, William gave some advice that I think rings true no matter what trait you have. He said: "Don't be afraid of being who you are or of making the best of it. Recognize your limitations and the challenges that you are going to face, by virtue of who you are. I believe that people can do amazing things if they set their mind to it. *Make the best of who you are.*"

I couldn't have put it better. I truly believe that each unique personality profile brings a wealth of ascendant strengths and positive characteristics. One of the real joys of being a psychiatrist is having the opportunity to meet people across the human spectrum and to learn about the incredible diversity of personalities that exists. I have yet to meet a person who couldn't make small changes in his or her life to better embrace their dominant trait(s). And I have yet to hear a story of a person who regretted making those small changes. The more comfortable you are with who you are, the better off you'll be.

That's why the central tenet of this book is *Know thyself.* I hope that through reading this book you have come to see yourself, your personality traits, your struggles, and your strengths in a new light. I hope you have come to some new insights about what it means to be mentally healthy and successful. And I hope you are now able to embrace your traits. Because you are indeed *Better Than Normal*—and that's all good!

APPENDIX: THE QUESTIONNAIRES

WITH THE ASSISTANCE of my colleague Dr. Jerry Whiteman, I have developed these eight questionnaires designed to help you understand your personality profile. By answering the questions in the pages that follow and calculating your score, you can determine which traits are dominant in your personality. You may already think you know what your dominant trait(s) is/are, but I encourage you to keep an open mind. You never know, you just may be in for a surprise.

A note of caution: These are not medical diagnostic tests, nor are they meant to take the place of a psychiatric assessment. Even if you are a ten-plus on a trait, do not despair! Ask yourself whether your trait is standing in the way of your ability to function on a daily basis. Does it interfere with your relationships, or affect your job or family in a negative way? If not, you may have already made the healthy life choices that allow you to embrace your trait. Dr. Whiteman and I both know "ten" scorers in various traits who live functional and happy lives without meds.

But if you feel strongly that your trait is seriously disabling to your life, then I encourage you to consider scheduling an appointment with a psychiatrist.

Also, understand that time and events may alter your scores somewhat, so take the tests more than once, especially when and if your life situation changes. You'll be amazed how your underlying trait profile may change a bit based on circumstances. Think of the knowledge that you gain from this book as part of an ongoing process of self-understanding. For more information, please visit my website, DrDaleArcher.com.

So please, respond to the questionnaires. Then use this profile as a resource to help you understand in greater depth the aspects of your personality that make you unique and the things you can do to embrace your dominant trait(s).

Adventurous (ADHD)

Rate yourself on the following scale:

NEVER				SOMETIMES					OFTEN
1	2	3	4	5	6	7	8	9	10

1. I can't decide what I want to do. _____

2. I have a hard time staying focused on a task. _____

3. I'm hyperactive. _____

4. I'm restless. _____

5. I quickly lose interest in many things I usually enjoy. _____

6. I am impulsive. _____

7. I try to do many things at once. _____

8. I feel I have a hundred things going through my mind. _____

9. I get bored easily. _____

10. I don't like waiting. _____

11. I sometimes act before thinking things through. _____

12. I'm not very organized. _____

TOTAL _____

Divide your total by 10 to get your ADHD score _____

Perfectionist (OCD)

Rate yourself on the following scale:

NEVER				SOMETIMES					OFTEN
1	2	3	4	5	6	7	8	9	10

1. I have thoughts that just won't go away. _____

2. I have a high level of anxiety about my ability to do things right. _____

3. People who know me think I'm a perfectionist. _____

4. I realize that some of my recurring thoughts are unreasonable. _____

5. I feel driven at times to perform various behaviors. _____

6. I arrange everything by size, shape, or color. _____

7. I have some rituals that won't make sense to someone watching me. _____

8. I need things to turn out "just right." _____

9. I just can't stand any type of mess. _____

10. I find that some of my behaviors actually interfere with getting things done. _____

11. I like everything very orderly. _____

12. I find I repeat myself just to make sure I get my point across. _____

TOTAL _____

Divide your total by 10 to get your OCD score _____

SHY (SOCIAL ANXIETY DISORDER)

Rate yourself on the following scale:

NEVER			SOMETIMES						OFTEN
1	2	3	4	5	6	7	8	9	10

1. I am nervous when meeting someone new. _____

2. I am anxious in everyday interactions with others. _____

3. I feel that I am being judged by others. _____

4. I believe that people are criticizing me behind my back. _____

5. I am very self-conscious. _____

6. I am shy. _____

7. I sweat a lot when I feel "on stage." _____

8. I become nauseous if I have to speak in public. _____

9. I feel my hands tremble or my muscles stiffen when talking to people. _____

10. I need to take something to relax (a drink or a pill) if I plan on being in a social situation. _____

11. I am easily embarrassed. _____

12. I dread going to new places where I don't know anybody. _____

TOTAL _____

Divide your total by 10 to get your social anxiety score _____

HYPER-ALERT (GENERALIZED ANXIETY DISORDER)

Rate yourself on the following scale:

NEVER				SOMETIMES					OFTEN
1	2	3	4	5	6	7	8	9	10

1. I am a worrier. _____

2. I am restless. _____

3. I get tired quickly, even after starting out feeling okay. _____

4. I'm on edge, even jumpy. _____

5. I'm easily upset when things don't go smoothly. _____

6. I have problems sleeping and resting. _____

7. I am stressed. _____

8. I have difficulty concentrating on even simple tasks. _____

9. People say I overanalyze things. _____

10. I believe I have more problems than other people. _____

11. I expect and plan for the worst. _____

12. I think about everything that could go wrong. _____

TOTAL _____

Divide your total by 10 to get your generalized anxiety score _____

DRAMATIC (HISTRIONIC)

Rate yourself on the following scale:

NEVER   SOMETIMES   OFTEN

1   2   3   4   5   6   7   8   9   10

1. I like to be noticed. _____

2. I dress in a way that causes people to look. _____

3. I show my emotions. _____

4. I speak in a way that causes others to listen. _____

5. If I'm feeling ill, I will let others hear about it. _____

6. I make decisions quickly. _____

7. I like for others to think I'm sexy. _____

8. I can put on a good show. _____

9. I don't mind breaking a few rules to get what I want. _____

10. I love to perform. _____

11. I like being the center of attention. _____

12. I am easily bored. _____

TOTAL _____

Divide your total by 10 to get your histrionic score _____

SELF-FOCUSED (NARCISSISTIC)

Rate yourself on the following scale:

NEVER				SOMETIMES					OFTEN
1	2	3	4	5	6	7	8	9	10

1. I enjoy telling people about my accomplishments. _____

2. I am sure that I am superior to most people due to my talents. _____

3. I have success far more than others my age. _____

4. I would make a "good catch" for a worthy person. _____

5. I am confident that I will have greater successes in life than most people will. _____

6. I rarely make mistakes. _____

7. I am aware that most people are jealous of me. _____

8. I deserve first-class treatment wherever I go. _____

9. I don't have time for stupid people. _____

10. I am unique and special. _____

11. I will do what is necessary to achieve my goal even if it means pushing others out of my way. _____

12. I am more attractive than most people. _____

TOTAL _____

Divide your total by 10 to get your narcissistic score _____

HIGH ENERGY (BIPOLAR)

Rate yourself on the following scale:

NEVER   SOMETIMES   OFTEN

1   2   3   4   5   6   7   8   9   10

1. I have mood swings from high to low.   _____

2. I often feel like I'm wired.   _____

3. I have problems concentrating.   _____

4. I have boundless energy.   _____

5. I have trouble sleeping.   _____

6. I don't need much sleep.   _____

7. I seem to make a lot of plans but often have problems finishing them.   _____

8. I often do things that I later regret.   _____

9. I have problems keeping focused on what I'm doing.   _____

10. I have racing thoughts.   _____

11. Other people get on my nerves.   _____

12. I am restless most of the time.   _____

TOTAL   _____

Divide your total by 10 to get your bipolar score   _____

MAGICAL (SCHIZOPHRENIA)

Rate yourself on the following scale:

NEVER				SOMETIMES					OFTEN
1	2	3	4	5	6	7	8	9	10

1. I believe in fate and destiny. _____

2. I have a sixth sense; I can sense
   when trouble is coming. _____

3. I have a good-luck charm that helps me deal
   with problems. _____

4. When I meet someone I can tell if he is good or evil. _____

5. I believe I am gifted in ways that
   other people don't understand. _____

6. I believe that I can tell when other people
   are not telling the truth. _____

7. I believe in God or a higher power. _____

8. I believe some people are born lucky and
   usually get all the breaks. _____

9. I hear or see things that others don't. _____

10. I have what others may call superstitions.
    But I believe in them. _____

11. I have found that if I wish for something
    long enough, it comes true. _____

12. I see miracles happening every day. _____

TOTAL _____

Divide your total by 10 to get your magical score _____

NOTES

ONE: THE EIGHT TRAITS

1. National Institute of Mental Health, "Statistics," www.nimh.nih.gov/health/topics/statistics/index.shtml.

2. "Prescription Drug Use Continues to Increase," *NCHS Data Brief 42* (September 2010), www.cdc.gov/nchs/data/databriefs/db42.pdf.

3. Robert Whitaker, *Anatomy of an Epidemic* (New York: Crown Publishers, 2010): 3.

4. Whitaker, *Anatomy,* 6.

5. Joel Lexchin et al., "Pharmaceutical Industry Sponsorship and Research Outcome and Quality: Systematic Review," *BMJ* (2003).

TWO: ADVENTUROUS

1. Mark Twain, *Adventures of Huckleberry Finn,* Electronic Text Center, University of Virginia Library. http://etext.virginia.edu/etcbin/toccer-new2?id=Twa2Huc.sgm&images=images/modeng&data=/texts/english/modeng/parsed&tag=public&part=1&division=div1.

2. B. Bloom, R. A. Cohen, and G. Freeman, "Summary Health Statistics for U.S. Children: National Health Interview Survey," 2008. National Center for Health Statistics, *Vital Health Stat* 10 (244) 2009: 66.

3. *60 Minutes* interview with Katie Couric, April 25, 2010.

4. Benedict Carey, "Forget What You Know about Study Habits," *New York Times* (September 6, 2010), www.nytimes.com/2010/09/07/health/views/07mind.html.

5. M. J. Rietveld, J. J. Hudziak, M. Bartels, C. E. van Beijsterveldt, and D. I. Boomsma, "Heritability of Attention Problems in Children: Longitudinal Results from a Study of Twins, Age 3 to 12," *Journal of Child Psychology and Psychiatry, and Allied Disciplines* 45 (March 2004): 577-88.

6. Chuansheng Chen et al., "Population Migration and the Variation of Dopamine D4 Receptor (DRD4) Allele Frequencies Around the Globe," *Evolution and Human Behavior* 21 (1999): 309.

7. Chuansheng Chen et al., 321.

8. "U. Va Researcher Probes ADHD's Effects on Safety of Young Drivers," *UVa Today* (January 31, 2008), www.virginia.edu/uvatoday/newsRelease.php?id=4033.

THREE: PERFECTIONIST

1. Anne M. Todd, *Vera Wang* (New York: Infobase Publishing, 2007): 75.

2. Thomas F. Oltmanns et al., *Case Studies in Abnormal Psychology* (Danvers, MA: John Wiley and Sons, 2007): 9.

3. Oltmanns et al., *Abnormal Psychology*, 7-8.

4. Ibid.

5. www.howiemandel.com/bio.html.

6. Joseph Polimeni, Jeffrey P. Reiss, and Jitender Sareen, "Could Obsessive-Compulsive Disorder Have Originated as a Group-Selected Adaptive Trait in Traditional Societies?" *Medical Hypotheses* (2005): 656.

7. Polimeni et al., "Obsessive Compulsive Disorder."

8. Ibid.

FOUR: SHY

1. Oltmanns et al., *Abnormal Psychology*, 53.

2. Shoshana Arbelle et al., "Relation of Shyness in Grade School Children to the Genotype for the Long Form of the Serotonin Transporter Promoter Region Polymorphism," *American Journal of Psychiatry* 160 (April 2003): 671-76.

3. Katharina Domschke and Udo Dannlowski, "Imaging Genetics of Anxiety Disorders," *NeuroImage* 53 (2010): 822-31.

4. Domschke and Dannlowski, 823.

5. Lisa M. McTeague et al., "Social Vision: Sustained Perceptual Enhancement of Affective Facial Cues in Social Anxiety," *NeuroImage* 54 (January 2011): 1615-24; Lora Rose Hunter, Julia D. Buckner, and Norman B. Schmidt, "Interpreting Facial Expressions: The Influence of Social Anxiety, Emotional Valence, and Race," *Journal of Anxiety Disorders* 23 (May 2009): 482-88.

6. David L. Sinn, Samuel D. Gosling, and Natalie A Moltschaniwskyj, "Development of Shy/Bold Behaviour in Squid: Context-Specific Phenotypes Associated with Developmental Plasticity," *Animal Behaviour* 75 (February 2008): 433-42.

7. Caroline Knapp, "Shy," *Salon* (March 5, 1999), www.salon.com/life/feature/1999/03/05feature.html.

8. Sharon Shiovitz-Ezra and Sara A. Leitsch, "The Role of Social Relationships in Predicting Loneliness," *National Association of Social Workers* (2010): 157.

9. John Cacioppo and William Patrick, *Loneliness: Human Nature and the Need for Social Connection* (New York: W. W. Norton & Co., 2008).

10. Sharon Shiovitz-Ezra and Sara A. Leitsch, "The Role of Social Relationships in Predicting Loneliness," *National Association of Social Workers* (2010): 157.

11. Knapp, "Shy."

12. Albert C. Bardi and Michael F. Brady, "Why Shy People Use Instant Messaging: Loneliness and Other Motives," *Computers in Human Behavior* 26 (November 2010): 1722-26.

FIVE: HYPER-ALERT

1. Oltsmanns et al., *Abnormal Psychology*, 26.

2. Association for Psychological Science, "A Little Anxiety Is Sometimes a Good Thing, Study Shows," *Science Daily* (April 5, 2008), www.sciencedaily.com/releases/2008/04/080403104350.htm.

SIX: DRAMATIC

1. Angie A. Kehagia, "Anaïs Nin: A Case Study of Personality Disorder and Creativity," *Personality and Individual Differences* 46 (2009): 801.

2. Ibid, 803.

3. Ibid, 801.

4. Paul S. Links and Michelle Stockwell, "Indications for Couple Therapy: The Paradox of the Histrionic/Obsessive-Compulsive Couple," *Journal of Family Psychotherapy* 15 (2004): 86.

5. Hwee S. Khoo and Giles St. J. Burch, "The 'Dark Side' of Leadership Personality and Transformational Leadership: An Exploratory Study," *Personality and Individual Differences* 44 (2008): 95.

SEVEN: SELF-FOCUSED

1. Seamus McGraw, "Sheen Demands 50% Raise for 'Two and a Half Men,'" *TODAY.com* (February 28, 2011, 7:32 p.m.), http://today.msnbc.msn.com/id/41824830/ns/today-entertainment.

2. Jeffrey Kluger, "Putting Bernie Madoff on The Couch," *Time* (December 31, 2008), www.time.com/time/health/article/0,8599,1869123,00.html.

3. Vince Calio, "Psychiatrist Reveals How to Spot Another Bernie Madoff," *International Business Times* (February 4, 2011), http.ibtimes.com/articles/109146/20110204/bernie-madoff-narcissism-ponzi-psychiatrists.htm.

4. Sigmund Karterud, "On Narcissism, Evolution, and Group Dynamics: A Tribute to Malcolm Pines," *Group Analysis* (September 2010): 305.

5. Ibid, 306.

6. Michael Maccoby, "Narcissistic Leaders: The Incredible Pros, the Inevitable Cons," *The Harvard Business Review* (January-February 2000), www.maccoby.com/Articles/NarLeaders.shtml.

7. Benedict Carey, "Narcissism: The Malady of Me," *New York Times* (December 4, 2010), www.nytimes.com/2010/12/05/weekinreview/05carey.html.

8. Pamela Paul, "From Students, Less Kindness for Strangers?" *New York Times* (June 25, 2010).

9. Soraya Mehdizadeh, "Self-Presentation 2.0: Narcissism and Self-Esteem on Facebook," *CyberPsychology, Behavior & Social Networking* (August 2010): 357-64.

EIGHT: HIGH ENERGY

1. Kay Redfield Jamison, *An Unquiet Mind* (New York: Random House, 1995): 68.

2. ——, *Touched with Fire* (New York: Free Press Paperback, 1994): 30.

3. ——, *Fire,* 29.

4. J. H. Barnett and J. W. Smoller, "The Genetics of Bipolar Disorder," *Neuroscience* (November 24, 2009): 331.

5. Oltmanns, *Abnormal Psychology,* 118.

6. Jamison, *Fire,* 4.

7. Ibid.

8. Benedict Carey, "Hypomanic? Absolutely. But Oh So Productive!" *New York Times* (March 22, 2005), http://query.nytimes.com/gst/fullpage.html?res=950DE3D61E3CF931A15750C0A9639C8B63&pagewanted=1.

9. G. St J. Burch, P. J. Corr, and C. Pavelis, "Schizotypy and Creativity in Visual Artists," *British Journal of Psychology* 97 (May 2006): 177-90.

10. "Sleep and Mental Health," *Harvard Mental Health Letter* (July 2009), http://www.health.harvard.edu/newsletters/Harvard_Mental_Health _Letter/2009/July/Sleep-and-mental-health.

11. Ibid.

NINE: MAGICAL

1. Benjamin Weiser, "In a Field of Reason, Lawyers Woo Luck Too," *New York Times* (February 17, 2011), www.nytimes.com/2011/02/18/ nyregion/18lawyers.html?_r=1&adxnnl=1&emc=eta1&pagewanted =2&adxnnlx=12980340794CEbfXoHgpHOBasbTG5aGQ.

2. Richard A. Van Dorn, Jeffrey W. Swanson, Eric B. Elbogen, and Marvin S. Swartz, "A Comparison of Stigmatizing Attitudes Toward Persons with Schizophrenia in Four Stakeholder Groups: Perceived Likelihood of Violence and Desire for Social Distance," *Psychiatry* 68 (2) (Summer 2005): 153.

3. Benedict Carey, "Talk Therapy Lifts Severe Schizophrenics," *New York Times* (October 4, 2011): D6.

4. Bernard Crespi, Kyle Summers, and Steve Dorus, *Adaptive Evolution of Genes Underlying Schizophrenia,* Proceedings of the Royal Society B (2007): 2801-10.

5. J. Polimeni and J. P. Reiss, "How Shamanism and Group Selection May Reveal the Origins of Schizophrenia," *Medical Hypotheses* (2002): 244-48.

6. Crespi et al., "Adaptive Evolution," 2806.

7. Eugene Subbotsky, "Magical Thinking: Reality or Illusion?" *The Psychologist* (June 2004): 336-39.

8. Rachel Miller and Joanne McCormack, "Faith and Religious Delusions in First-Episode Schizophrenia," *Social Work in Mental Health* (December 1, 2006): 39.

9. ——, "Faith and Religious Delusions," 44-47.

10. Neale Donald Walsch, *Conversations with God: An Uncommon Dialogue* (New York: G. P. Putnam's Sons, 1996): 6.

CONCLUSION

1. Gardiner Harris, "Talk Doesn't Pay, So Psychiatry Turns Instead to Drug Therapy," *New York Times* (March 5, 2011), www.nytimes .com/2011/03/06/health/policy/06doctors.html?pagewanted=1&ref =homepage&src=me.

BIBLIOGRAPHY

Arbelle, Shoshana et al. "Relation of Shyness in Grade School Children to the Genotype for the Long Form of the Serotonin Transporter Promoter Region Polymorphism." *American Journal of Psychiatry* 160 (April 2003): 671–76.

Association for Psychological Science. "A Little Anxiety Is Sometimes A Good Thing, Study Shows." *Science Daily* (April 5, 2008), www .sciencedaily.com/releases/2008/04/080403104350.htm.

Bardi, Albert C., and Michael F. Brady. "Why Shy People Use Instant Messaging: Loneliness and Other Motives." *Computers in Human Behavior* 26 (November 2010): 1722–26.

Barnett, J. H., and J. W. Smoller. "The Genetics of Bipolar Disorder." *Neuroscience* (November 24, 2009): 331–43.

Blade87. Comment on Schwartz, Casey. "Busting the Adderall Myth." *The Daily Beast* (December 21, 2010), http.thedailybeast.com/blogs-and-stories/2010-12-21/adderall-concentration-benefits-in-doubt-new-study/?cid=hp:mainpromo7.

Bloom, B., R. A. Cohen, and G. Freeman. "Summary Health Statistics for U.S. Children: National Health Interview Survey." 2008. *National Center for Health Statistics, Vital Health Stat* 10 (244): 2009–66.

Cacioppo, John, and William Patrick. *Loneliness: Human Nature and the Need for Social Connection.* New York: W. W. Norton & Co., 2008.

Calio, Vince. "Psychiatrist Reveals How to Spot Another Bernie Madoff."

International Business Times (February 4, 2011), http.ibtimes.com/articles/109146/20110204/bernie-madoff-narcissism-ponzi-psychiatrists.htm.

Carey, Benedict. "Forget What You Know About Study Habits." *New York Times* (September 6, 2010), www.nytimes.com/2010/09/07/health/views/07mind.html.

———. "Narcissism: The Malady of Me." *New York Times* (December 4, 2010), www.nytimes.com/2010/12/05/weekinreview/05carey.html.

———. "Talk Therapy Lifts Severe Schizophrenics," *New York Times* (October 4, 2011): D6.

Chuansheng, Chen et al. "Population Migration and the Variation of Dopamine D4 Receptor (DRD4) Allele Frequencies Around the Globe." *Evolution and Human Behavior* 21 (1999): 309-24.

Crespi, Bernard, Kyle Summers, and Steve Dorus. "Adaptive Evolution of Genes Underlying Schizophrenia." *Proceedings of the Royal Society B* (2007): 2801-10.

Domschke, Katharina, and Udo Dannlowski. "Imaging Genetics of Anxiety Disorders." *NeuroImage* 53 (2010): 822-31.

Ellwood, Mark. "The Crying Game." *New York Times Magazine* (March 9, 2008).

Gartner, John. *The Hypomanic Edge.* New York: Simon & Schuster, 2005.

Greenberg, Gary. "The Book of Woe." *Wired* (January 2011): 128-36.

Harris, Gardiner. "Talk Doesn't Pay, So Psychiatry Turns Instead to Drug Therapy." *New York Times* (March 5, 2011), www.nytimes.com/2011/03/06/health/policy/06doctors.html?pagewanted=1&ref=homepage&src=me.

Hartmann, Thom. *The Edison Gene.* Rochester, VT: Park Street Press, 2003.

www.howiemandel.com/bio.html.

Hunter, Lora Rose, Julia D. Buckner, and Norman B. Schmidt. "Interpreting Facial Expressions: The Influence of Social Anxiety, Emotional Valence, and Race." *Journal of Anxiety Disorders* 23 (May 2009): 482-88.

Jamison, Kay Redfield. *An Unquiet Mind.* New York: Random House, 1995.

——. *Touched with Fire.* New York: Free Press Paperback, 1994.

Karterud, Sigmund. "On Narcissism, Evolution, and Group Dynamics: A Tribute to Malcolm Pines," *Group Analysis* (September 2010): 301-10.

Kehagia, Angie A. "Anaïs Nin: A Case Study of Personality Disorder and Creativity." *Personality and Individual Differences* 46 (2009): 800-08.

Khoo, Hwee S., and Giles St. J. Burch. "The 'Dark Side' of Leadership Personality and Transformational Leadership: An Exploratory Study." *Personality and Individual Differences* 44 (2008): 86-97.

Kluger, Jeffrey. "Putting Bernie Madoff on the Couch." *Time* (December 31, 2008), www.time.com/time/health/article/0,8599,1869123,00.html.

Knapp, Caroline. "Shy." *Salon* (March 5, 1999), www.salon.com/life/feature/1999/03/05feature.html.

Lexchin, Joel et al. "Pharmaceutical Industry Sponsorship and Research Outcome and Quality: Systematic Review." *BMJ* (2003).

Links, Paul S., and Michelle Stockwell. "Indications for Couple Therapy: The Paradox of the Histrionic/Obsessive-Compulsive Couple." *Journal of Family Psychotherapy* 15 (4) 2004: 73-88.

Maccoby, Michael. "Narcissistic Leaders: The Incredible Pros, the Inevitable Cons." *The Harvard Business Review* (January–February, 2000), www.maccoby.com/Articles/NarLeaders.shtml.

McGraw, Seamus. "Sheen Demands 50% Raise for 'Two and a Half Men.'" *TODAY.com* (February 28, 2011, 7:32 p.m.), http://today.msnbc.msn.com/id/41824830/ns/today-entertainment.

McTeague, Lisa M. et al. "Social Vision: Sustained Perceptual Enhancement of Affective Facial Cues in Social Anxiety." *NeuroImage* 54 (January 2011): 1615-24.

Mehdizadeh, Soraya. "Self-Presentation 2.0: Narcissism and Self-Esteem on Facebook." *CyberPsychology, Behavior & Social Networking* (August 2010): 357-64.

Miller, Rachel, and Joanne McCormack. "Faith and Religious Delusions in First-Episode Schizophrenia." *Social Work in Mental Health* (December 1, 2006): 37-50.

National Institute of Mental Health. "Statistics," www.nimh.nih.gov/health/topics/statistics/index.shtml.

Oltmanns, Thomas F. et al. *Case Studies in Abnormal Psychology.* Danvers, MA: John Wiley and Sons, 2007.

Paul, Pamela. "From Students, Less Kindness for Strangers?" *New York Times* (June 25, 2010).

Polimeni, Joseph, Jeffrey P. Reiss, and Jitender Sareen. "Could Obsessive-Compulsive Disorder Have Originated as a Group-Selected Adaptive Trait in Traditional Societies?" *Medical Hypotheses* (2005).

Polimeni, J., and J. P. Reiss. "How Shamanism and Group Selection May Reveal the Origins of Schizophrenia." *Medical Hypotheses* (2002): 244-48.

"Prescription Drug Use Continues to Increase." NCHS Data Brief 42 (September 2010), www.cdc.gov/nchs/data/databriefs/db42.pdf.

Shiovitz-Ezra, Sharon, and Sara A. Leitsch. "The Role of Social Relationships in Predicting Loneliness." *National Association of Social Workers* (2010).

Sinn, David L., Samuel D. Gosling, and Natalie A Moltschaniwskyj. "Development of Shy/Bold Behaviour in Squid: Context-Specific Phenotypes Associated with Developmental Plasticity." *Animal Behaviour* 75 (February 2008): 433-42.

60 Minutes, CBS News, interview with Katie Couric, April 25, 2010.

"Sleep and Mental Health." *Harvard Mental Health Letter* (July 2009), www.health.harvard.edu/newsletters/Harvard_Mental_Health_Letter/2009/July/Sleep-and-mental-health.

St J. Burch, Giles, P. J. Corr, and C. Pavelis, "Schizotypy and Creativity in Visual Artists," *British Journal of Psychology* 97 (May 2006): 177-90.

Subbotsky, Eugene. "Magical Thinking: Reality or Illusion?" *The Psychologist* (June 2004): 336-39.

Todd, Anne M. *Vera Wang.* New York: Infobase Publishing, 2007.

Twain, Mark. *Adventures of Huckleberry Finn.* Electronic Text Center, University of Virginia Library, http://etext.virginia.edu/etcbin/toccer

-new2?id=Twa2Huc.sgm&images=images/modeng&data=/texts/english/modeng/parsed&tag=public&part=1&division=div1.

"U. Va Researcher Probes ADHD's Effects on Safety of Young Drivers." *UVa Today* (January 31, 2008), www.virginia.edu/uvatoday/newsRelease.php?id=4033.

Van Dorn, Richard A., Jeffrey W. Swanson, Eric B. Elbogen, and Marvin S. Swartz. "A Comparison of Stigmatizing Attitudes Toward Persons with Schizophrenia in Four Stakeholder Groups: Perceived Likelihood of Violence and Desire for Social Distance." *Psychiatry* 68 (2) (Summer 2005): 153.

Walsch, Neale Donald. *Conversations with God: An Uncommon Dialogue.* New York: G. P. Putnam's Sons, 1996.

Weiser, Benjamin. "In a Field of Reason, Lawyers Woo Luck Too" *New York Times* (February 17, 2011), http.nytimes.com/2011/02/18/nyregion/18lawyers.html?_r=1&adxnnl=1&emc=eta1&pagewanted=2&adxnnlx=1298034079-4CEbfXoHgpHOBasbTG5aGQ.

Whitaker, Robert. *Anatomy of an Epidemic.* New York: Crown Publishers, 2010.

ACKNOWLEDGMENTS

THERE ARE SO MANY PEOPLE to thank that the hardest part has been deciding on the best way to organize the acknowledgments, so I've opted for the simplest: chronological order. The list includes folks that have helped with my career, website, clinical practice, and TV engagements, as well as with the book itself. All of those ventures generated and shaped the ideas that are articulated here.

Here goes.

In college, my thesis adviser, the professor of philosophy Dr. Michael Zimmerman, suggested that gaining a doctorate in philosophy and spending my life as a university professor would not be the best use of my talents. He recommended medical school and a focus on psychiatry instead. It took me four years to realize he was right. I still wonder, "How could he know that?" Maybe I'm not as complicated as I think I am?

At Tulane Medical School my adviser, Dr. Dean Ellithorpe, also suggested psychiatry, even though I was sure that internal medicine was right for me. At least it only took me a year to realize I was wrong and follow my teacher's advice.

I thank Dr. Emilio Romero for teaching me the art and science of psychotherapy, and Dr. Ray Faber for teaching me the art and science of biological psychiatry. This was back in the day when psychiatric training focused equally on therapy and medication.

We desperately need to get back to that approach in training our young psychiatrists.

I thank Elton Williams, past president of Lake Charles Memorial Hospital, who asked me to found a forty-bed psychiatric unit at the hospital. Thanks to Larry Graham, the current CEO of Lake Charles Memorial Hospital, who gave me the support and allowed the time to put this book together and to pursue the media ventures that are such a big part of the effort.

Thanks to the psychiatrists affiliated with the Institute for Neuropsychiatry: Dr. Kashinath Yadalam, Dr. Charles Murphy, III, Dr. Said Cantu, Dr. Sreelatha Pulakhandam, Dr. Ramin Shala, and Dr. Vidushi Babber. To the clinical staff of the Institute for Neuropsychiatry: Dr. Jerry Whiteman, Sarah Hairgrove, Lloyd Kelley, Molly Larson, Jeanne Wolfe, Sheila Gilley, Art Schafer, Larry Cupit, Lea Ann Dauphine, Retha Fontenot, and Sharon Jacko. Also to the support staff: Patsy Johnson, Tammy Turner, Dorothy Rogers, Pam Espey, Mandy Powers, Charlene Racca, Debbie Jardell, Petra Mallett, Amanda McCown, Raegan Miller, Jada Redmond, Mali Gnu, and Kaley Cooling.

Thanks to Sonja Clarke, who was instrumental in the early brainstorming and the launching of my website in collaboration with John Munsell and his team from Bizzuka. Paul Chaney for his work with me on all Web-related matters; to the team for the original Dr. Dale Archer Show: Patsy Johnson, Sarah Hairgrove, Tammy Turner, Patrice Michon, Kandi Misenar, Chuck Boudreaux, Hal Comeaux, Marty Myers, Justin Toney, Gary Mutchler; and to all those who have helped me get my message out to the world over the last several years: Kristy Armand, Christine Fisher, Adam Weiss, Brian Strong, and Annie Scranton.

Thanks to Jane Velez-Mitchell, who gave me my first national TV appearance, and the entire staff of her show *Issues with Jane Velez-Mitchell,* including Cameron Baird, Leslie Tucker, Amy

Doyle, Alicia Johnson, and the rest of the team. Other great TV people who have helped: Perry Sanders, Monty Seward, Peter Cascone, Catherine Hickland, Dr. Lillian Glass, Todd Reynolds, Lynne Jordal-Martin, Jordan Chariton, Lis Wiehl, Kimberly Guilfoyle, and of course my fantastic agent, Ashley Davis with CAA, who took a chance on an unknown guy.

On to the book itself. Thanks to: Mary Hall Mayer for insisting I write this book sooner rather than later and referring me to Madeleine Morel, who introduced me to my literary agents, Todd Shuster and Jennifer Gates of Zachary, Shuster, Harmsworth. I can't imagine working with any other agents—you two are the best!

Nicole Mackey for helping to define the original "Eight Traits of Greatness" and donating many hours to the effort, and Dr. Jerry Whiteman for his help with the questionnaires.

Maggie Greenwood-Robinson for her help with the original proposal.

John Butman (who I swear can read my mind) and his team, Hannah Alpert-Abrams and Anna Weiss, from Idea Platforms, Inc., for all of the incredible research, structure, and help with the text they provided.

My editor, Sydny Miner at Random House (and her right hand, Anna Thompson), who understood immediately what I was trying to say and gave me the platform to say it. Thanks for making this book so much easier, Sydny. Crown Archetype publisher Tina Constable, along with Tammy Blake, Ellen Folan, Meredith McGinnis, Christina Foxley, Robert Siek, Norman Watkins, Jen O'Connor, Elina Nudelman, and everyone else at Crown who helped make this book a reality. And of course Gretchen Crary, Dee Dee De Bartlo, Kim Cowser, and the rest of the team at February Partners.

A special thanks to Patsy Johnson, who started as my sole employee in 1987 and now is the vice president at the Institute for Neuropsychiatry. You've been involved in all of it, twenty-four years and counting, and none of this would have been possible without you.

Finally, and most important, thanks to my very close-knit family: my father, Dr. Dale Archer Sr., and mother, Val, who have been married for fifty-five years and are still going strong—you two have been my source of stability throughout this long, strange journey. My sister, Lee, an amazing person—how you have put up with me all these years I'll never know, but thanks. My daughter, Adri, who's turned her phenomenal OCD trait into a successful career in New York, and my son, Trey, who as of this writing is backpacking the Silk Road between China and Europe (ADHD and loving it!).

All the credit is yours; any mistakes are mine.

INDEX

Cajun culture, 195
Caldwell, Gail, 88
calmness: self-focused trait and, 142
Calvin (comic strip character), 35
camera story, Kurt's, 68-69, 70
Campbell, Joseph, 120
cancer, 62, 100
car accidents, 50
careers. *See* work/careers
caring: shy trait and, 83
Carnegie, Andrew, 36, 167
causation: eight traits and, 23
charm/charisma
    dramatic trait and, 120, 128
    high-energy trait and, 172
    self-focused trait and, 130, 147-48, 149,
        151
cheating: in relationships, 124-26
checking, obsessive, 63
Chemical Imbalance Depression (Archer),
    4
chemical imbalances: as cause of mental
    disorders, 17
chimpanzees: narcissism among, 139
Chocolat (movie), 197
Christie, Agatha, 36, 78
chronic pain, 100
clock repairman: perfectionist trait and,
    66-67
cognitive therapy, 61, 77, 163
Columbus, Christopher, 36, 167, 168
Combs, Sean, 176
compassion, 178
compulsions
    definition of, 59-60
    as method for dealing with obsessions,
        59-60
    See also obsessive-compulsive disorder
computer nerds: shyness of, 78-79
confidence
    adventurous trait and, 43
    dramatic trait and, 128
    high-energy trait and, 169, 173
    hyper-alert trait and, 96, 97
    importance of, 42
    magical trait and, 177, 189
    self-focused trait and, 133, 136, 138,
        141, 149, 151, 205
    shy trait and, 81, 90
continuum model
    mild-traited people and, 206
    multi-traited people and, 205-6

overview of, 22-31
    See also specific trait
Conversations with God series (Walsch),
    193
coping: magical trait and, 193-95
Courtney (high-energy person), 30-31
creativity
    adventurous trait and, 53
    high-energy trait and, 164, 170, 172, 175
    magical trait and, 182, 187, 188, 198
    schizophrenia and, 182, 187
criminals: self-focused trait and, 134
Cruise, Tom, 110
cyclothymia (bipolar II disorder), 158-59

dating
    online, 89, 197
    speed, 197
Debra (shy person), 75-76, 77
decision making
    dramatic trait and, 112
    magical trait and, 190, 198
    OCD and, 204
    shy trait and, 82
Depp, Johnny, 197
depression
    anxiety and, 95, 97
    bipolar disorder and, 159
    as "common cold of psychiatry," 24
    diagnosis of mental disorders and, 200
    dramatic trait and, 113
    eight traits and, 23-24
    high-energy trait and, 26, 155, 171
    HPD and, 117
    hyper-alert trait and, 95
    OCD and, 60
    prevalence of, 6, 7-8
    self-focused trait and, 31, 142
    stigmatizing of, 3-4, 6
    treatment for, 3, 4, 7-8, 18
detective: as perfectionists, 58
*Diagnostic and Statistical Manual of
    Mental Disorders* (DSM)
    ADHD and, 22, 38, 39
    eight traits and, 16, 22
    HPD and, 115-17
    hypomania and, 158, 164
    making the most of dominant traits
        and, 205
    narcissistic personality disorder and,
        22, 135, 139
    OCD and, 22, 57, 59